⚵ CEREMONIES FOR REAL LIFE ⚵

CEREMONIES FOR REAL LIFE

CARINE FABIUS

WILDCAT CANYON PRESS
An imprint of Council Oak Books, LLC
San Francisco/Tulsa

Ceremonies for Real Life
©2003 by Carine Fabius

Book design: Shannon Laskey
Cover design: Mary Beth Salmon

Printed in Canada

Council Oak Books, LLC
2105 E. 15th Street, Ste. B
Tulsa, OK 74104

ISBN 1-885171-65-X

Library of Congress Cataloging-in-Publication Data

Fabius, Carine.
   Ceremonies for real life / by Carine Fabius.
      p. cm.
   Includes bibliographical references.
   ISBN 1-885171-65-x
    1. Rites and ceremonies. I. Title.

BL600.F33 2001
291.3'8--dc21

                    2001046901

For my teacher, Maharaji
whose loving guidance makes my ride through
this life a smoother, more enjoyable journey

&CONTENTS &

❧ ACKNOWLEDGMENTS ❧

I would like to thank Jillian Hessel-Spivak, whose epiphany about the necessity of this book was the force that fueled its creation. Her loving presence, support and generosity over the years, I hold close to my heart. I would also like to thank the goddess Saraswati, patron deity for writers, musicians and artists, for her constant inspiration throughout the writing of this book. To my dear friends and ceremony sisters, Jeannie Winston and Kathryn Takis, thank you for your presence in my life; and double thanks, Jeannie, for the wonderful illustrations you created for the book! Warm thanks to Linda Winters, whose support and advice in the area of publishing gave me direction and renewed purpose when I needed it most. To Henrietta Cosentino, thank you so much for the helpful and timely article you sent my way. Special thanks to Tamara Traeder, Carol Brown and Roy Carlisle of Wildcat Canyon Press for championing this book. Heartfelt appreciation goes to Paulette Millichap and Ja-lene Clark of Council Oak Books for the consciousness they bring to the work they do, for their kindness, and for letting me have my way! I thank my mother and father, Mireille and Claude Fabius for their belief in my abilities as a writer and for their unwavering support of this project. And last but not least, I thank my husband, Pascal Giacomini, for being my best cheerleader and constant reminder that the show will go on!

INTRODUCTION

Over the years, beginning at a fairly young age, I have reflected on destiny. Fate. Is it prewritten—all laid out in a neat, straightforward, and unforgiving pattern? Or do free will, choice, and prayer make any difference at all in how our lives play out? Films, books, and true anecdotes that tackle the subject fascinate me: love derailed because of a lost letter; opportunity missed thanks to misunderstanding; fortune lost or made on the basis of a hunch. And what of luck? Timing? And the big one—karma?

Not long ago, I got up in the morning, dressed, hopped into my car and drove thirty minutes across town to my acupuncture appointment, only to be greeted by a blank look on my doctor's face. My appointment was for the same time, the next day. I was having a particularly busy week and could ill-afford to waste the time. But, as I navigated through thick, mid-morning traffic, rather than fume, I found myself wondering about how this seemingly unnecessary trip might be affecting my life. Was there some comment I might have overheard my husband make to someone on the phone that might have sparked a conversation that might have . . . ? Or, better yet, was it necessary for me to drive down those particular streets at these exact times in order for someone else's life to take a different turn? Perhaps a pedestrian or driver in the next lane might see me and be reminded of someone or something, which might prompt him to . . . ? As I said, I think about this stuff all the time.

I remember reeling from *Sliding Doors*, the movie in which the main character's life unfolds in two distinct styles based on a missed train. As the story develops, the woman who misses the train continues to live out the life she might have lived, while the life of the woman who makes the train takes a decidedly different turn.

Through a clever plot twist, one of the characters gets a new, short haircut, which makes it easy for the viewer to know whose life is currently playing out on the screen. At the film's denouement, though they've taken different roads, both women end up with the same guy! This really threw me. Did this mean that no matter what we go through or how we do it, we're fated to reach the same end? Although enjoyable as a film, the message left me somewhat deflated. And then I realized, Wait a minute, this is just a movie; and it is only this writer's take on the subject! Embarrassingly enough, it took that long and that movie to show me where I stood on the matter.

By now you may be wondering, what's the point? And what does all this have to do with ceremony? Well, the point is, that after all my musings on the subject, I have come to certain conclusions:

• That when we are in a conscious state—and by conscious I mean not stressed, confused, scared, or flustered, but present and centered—we always make the right decisions. And that goes for decisions that affect our lives or the lives of others. We make perfect choices, which sublimely weave themselves into a tapestry which I'm convinced is ever changing, ever evolving, and totally spontaneous, based on our thoughts, feelings, words, and actions.

• I believe in magic—the miraculous and delicious "anything-is-possible" nature of this life. I believe in the power of nature, of all the elements, of the stars and planets, and of their influence on human beings. And I believe in God, the unexplainable and beautiful force, which exists in all living things and which binds us all together into one organism that feeds off itself (or one another), creating reactions and mechanisms that vary depending on our consciousness.

• When we create and perform ceremonies, we consciously choose to put ourselves in a fully centered state. We choose to align ourselves with the forces of nature through our intention. We fully and presently take part in directing the flow of magic already at work in the ever-expanding and accommodating tapestry that creates itself as we live.

Performing ceremonies makes me feel like I have a say in how my life turns out. It makes me feel like I have some form of control of how it unfolds. This is not to say that everything works out exactly how I expect it to or according to my plans. Taking part in a ceremony means I am asking for help. I put in my request, back it up with the power of my creative intention, and then I try to surrender to the weave already in progress. At least when I am clever, I surrender. Because how I get there or how quickly I arrive is best left in more experienced hands!

CEREMONY

A Celebration of Life

When I turned sixteen, my mother decided my sweet sixteen party should be special, different from all the others. She suggested that everyone wear fancy gowns, and she turned the basement of our New York home into a glittering, candlelit ballroom. Ten tables for four were set with china and gleaming silverware; place cards told my friends where they should sit. My mother and two older sisters functioned as waitresses for the evening. They brought platters filled with mouth-watering Haitian specialties, poured soda pop in wine glasses, and tended to our every need. When time came, my elaborately decorated birthday cake, sixteen candles flaming, was brought slowly down the steps in dramatic fashion by one of my sisters, giving everyone the cue to stand up and sing to me. After the cake was eaten and the tables and chairs cleared, we danced the night away like regular teenagers—well, almost. We were teenagers who had experienced a formality, graciousness, and maturity for having been treated like distinguished adults. We all grew up a little that night, and for years many of my friends recalled this unique celebration with fondness.

Right around that time, just before turning sixteen, I got my period. Finally. By then, everyone around me had already been blessed with "the curse" for years, and I was sure I was abnormal. According to stories I'd heard, because of this abnormality, I was going to die soon. So, when I discovered the red stain in my underwear, I was ecstatic. Flooded with relief, I walked down the stairs to find my mother. She is a fashion designer, and she had set up shop in our basement. She was chatting with visiting friends when I called her from the kitchen upstairs. When I told her the news, a smile slowly spread on her face and she said, "There's a box of Kotex pads in the bathroom; you know what to do, right?" I nodded though I wasn't sure. I turned away hurriedly, but stopped short and called her back. "Don't go telling everyone downstairs, all right?" She promised she wouldn't. I went back to the bathroom, stuffed the thick pad in my underwear, and went back down to the basement to join my mother and her friends. When I stepped into the room, all eyes turned and every single woman in the room smiled sweetly at me, but they kept their mouths shut. Aaargh! Later that night, my grandmother, who lived with us, squeezed a five-dollar bill into my hand as she passed me in the dining room. "What's this for?" I said. She looked at me sternly and said, "You're a woman now." Then she walked away.

Those two stories stand out in my mind because in one instance, turning sixteen had been transformed into an unforgettable, exceptional, and momentous event in my life, whereas my First Blood had been treated as the equivalent of getting an A on a test. Maybe my sixteenth birthday party was the catalyst for my still-evolving love affair with ceremony; maybe it was the lack of ceremony surrounding an event that all at once gave me back my life, turned me into a woman, and allowed me to be like everyone else. I'm not sure. But I am sure that although we don't practice the art of ceremony nowadays, there is something in us that misses it. How do I know that? Because without realizing it, we do it all the time. Planning a party, preparing a meal, feasting, commiserating with friends, showing support—whenever people come together with love in their hearts, with intent to accomplish a goal, there is a gathering up of energies that takes place. This type of gathering is ceremonial in nature, and it feels good.

Everybody loves a good wedding. Why? Because they are emotional affairs, where strong feelings of love, commitment to union, and vows of support are being talked about and affirmed. For those people in attendance, hearts fill with good wishes for the couple, and tears of joy bubble up to the surface, enveloping everyone in a cloud of combined hopes. Ceremony at its best! But aside from those few, often traditional and religious ceremonies—marriage, first communion, bar mitzvah, etc.—very little else is celebrated in ceremonial fashion.

What if anniversary celebrations involved couples taking the time to focus on why they came together to begin with? Committing to each other all over again? Inviting friends to public re-affirmation rites that include them in a meaningful way? What would happen to our rising divorce rate?

In the middle of my thirty-ninth birthday party, I stopped the clock for a minute and asked everyone to tell me what they wished me most for my birthday. I did this because I believe that truly felt wishes do come to pass. One by one, my friends wished me the things they knew I wanted most. It was a beautiful and touching moment. Even my no-nonsense friends joined in, becoming emotional and teary in the process. Looking back on that time, I dare say that many of those wonderful wishes did materialize! Because of this, I propose turning the commonplace events of our lives into commemorative celebrations; drawing on them as boosters for kick-starting changes and growth opportunities, and using them as impetus to become transformed.

Hillary Clinton's notion that "it takes a village" is not just a political concept to be praised or ridiculed as befits personal ideology. Community is a powerful force. Let's bring that community of friends, family, and relations together; use that great energy to propel life into positive, forward motion; and watch what happens.

Years ago I offered to host a wedding shower in my home for my friend Jillian, but I warned her:

"I'm not into shower games, okay? I want to do something different."

"Like what?" she said.

"Like some kind of ceremony," I said. "Something that will celebrate the spirit of love and your union with Arthur, and matrimony."

"Sounds great!" she said.

So I set about researching which gods and goddesses, which herbs, oils, colors, and symbols are associated with love. I read up on rituals from different cultures and came up with my own. We had a wonderful time that afternoon, and to this day, Jillian reminds me of how special it was for her. Years later I offered to host her baby shower and reminded her that I still didn't want to play traditional games. In fact, over the years, I have often missed my friends' showers—not because I don't love them or want to support the important events in their lives, but because I feel those events are made superficial by the loss of original intent. Jillian and Arthur's baby shower was a co-ed affair, where people who wouldn't typically take part in any kind of ceremony—save a wedding or religious practice—found themselves completely involved with the process. Why? It felt good. We were there not just to bring baby presents and to eat, we were there to celebrate the arrival of a new member of our community, to put all our good wishes behind its safe delivery, to wish it good health and all the things we want most in life for our children. We had also gathered to give this new child's parents our pledge of support and help as they embarked on this new, important journey; to wish them strength and well-being, and to call upon all the powers in nature to help make our best wishes a reality.

It is said that thoughts are creative, that whatever we focus on, we attract. Ceremony is a time for us to harness the power of our minds and hearts to create wonderful, magical lives for ourselves and the people we love. To most of us in the western world, clear-cut divisions exist between the material and spiritual, the natural and supernatural, reality and imagination. But in most tribal and indigenous cultures, this is an alien concept. For those who live in close contact with nature, to imagine something is to make it real.

CEREMONY AS LINK TO THE DIVINE

It has been said that God conceptualized and created human beings in order to experience his full glory in the flesh. If this is true, then can it not be said that we created God by virtue of our need to experience the glory of our own divinity? In the same way, when we invoke and make appropriate offerings to a deity in a ceremonial setting, by the very power of our desire, we give that deity form and the characteristics by which we recognize him or her.

All elements of ceremony serve as focal points for communication with the divine. Sometimes they serve as go-between. For example, an atheist may not feel comfortable praying to God for patience; however she may be perfectly willing to wear a necklace of light-blue stones, since the blue ray imparts this virtue. Does it matter whether she prays or wears the necklace since God is said to reside in everything, even the tiniest speck of dust? I say whatever gets you there, go for it. If it's a prayer to Jesus, pray on. If it is a call to Buddha, make that call. And if the way you talk to your higher self about financial difficulty is by lighting a green candle inscribed with a symbol for Jupiter (for removal of debt) and Mercury (for riches), light that flame.

According to Haitians, it doesn't matter if you believe in the spirits of Vodou, as long as you serve them.

Ceremony can be done alone, with two people, or however many the situation or desire calls for. Ceremony is also a time to appreciate the power of stillness. Oftentimes during the course of a ritual, participants are asked to consider a color or to concentrate on the light of a candle. They might be asked to clear the mind of all thoughts, and to let go of current worries as they become cleansed through the use of sage or other purifying agents. Silence is powerful because it is one with the vibration of life. It is the force within that imparts information, generates gratitude, and promotes bliss. Silence also reminds us of our personal strength. According to Malidoma Patrice Somé, a renowned African shaman, "This is why the tree, the stone, the river and the mountain are quiet."

EMBRACING LIFE THROUGH CEREMONY

Why might people feel funny about performing rituals? The religious establishment, along with the intellectual establishment, has convinced us that non-traditional rituals or those not sanctioned by the church belong to primitive cultures—images of witchcraft come to mind. In my own country, Haiti, where Vodou ceremonies are performed daily by "the poor, uneducated masses," the ruling class tries hard to distance itself from such "pagan" practices. But Haitian history teaches that before launching an all-out massive attack against their oppressors, the African slaves performed a special ceremony during which they became possessed by the warrior spirits of Vodou. The odds were totally against them, but they saw themselves as gods—fearless, all-powerful, able to conquer all— and they won their freedom from the French.

I don't advocate the practice of Vodou or any other religion. Mostly I speak to the value of ritual and ceremony in diverse cultures throughout the world.

All of nature—the sun, the moon, animals, insects, birds, flowers, plants, and trees—have performed the same rituals of rising and setting, waxing and waning, pollinating and fertilizing, healing and growing, living and dying again and again since the beginning of time. So have we. Why not take time to find hidden meaning in the small ceremonies and rituals we perform every day on a conscious and subconscious level? Why not honor and appreciate these rituals for the way they enrich our lives?

To ritualize is to declare our connection with nature. There is nothing weird about participating in a ceremony. Think of it as getting back in touch with your true nature. Think of the Japanese and their elaborate tea ceremonies, or of Native Americans with their tribal practices. Remember the ceremonial way in which young men and women are taught to behave in military service in order to serve their country. And how about the ceremonial aspect of "spring cleaning," which is rooted in letting go of the old in order to make room for the new? Most people are delighted to be invited to a ceremony. Human beings love new experiences, things exotic and fresh. But they love ancient things even more. I would say that, as I found when performimg ceremonies for my friends, as host, you might be the ceremony's most celebrated person of all!

THINK OF CEREMONY AS ART

Like art, ritual involves spontaneity and the acknowledgement of established patterns of expression.

Art nourishes the soul, gives us pause, and inspires us. It transports us to other realms via the artist's imagination combined with our own, and adds beauty to our immediate environment. Art can also scandalize, cause controversy, and offend. Like art, ceremony has the power to transform and transport. It is up to us how we choose to direct our energies to create change in our lives. To that end, it can safely be said that creating ceremony is performance art at its most spontaneous and humble best!

Performance is the melding together of spectator and spectacle.

Like art, ritual performance or ceremony effects transformation in a way no other medium can in that it establishes communication with the unseen. In so doing, it provides efficient, personal translation for that which is otherwise difficult to grasp precisely because of its intangible nature.

Most people do not consider themselves artists, but being one is not an impossible, romantic dream. Create a ceremony and accept the acclaim usually reserved for the artistically gifted, for you will have created living, breathing art at its highest level.

THINK OF CEREMONY AS HELPING THE ENVIRONMENT

I believe that our present-day ecological crisis is due in part to a decline in ceremonies that link human beings to their environment. If we were in sync with, and thankful for the gifts we have—like our oceans, rivers, the air we breathe—perhaps we would take better care of them. Reviving the art of ceremony, indirectly and without fanfare, helps us recognize the elements commonly used in rituals. For example, the use of water, flowers, plants, and trees increases our awareness of their bountiful healing and magical properties. This awareness helps us appreciate and acknowledge the blessings heaped upon us by Mother Nature, free of charge, every day. To appreciate is to hold dear.

CREATING CEREMONIES

Why is such a fuss made over the age of sixteen? Why not seventeen? Besides the obvious passage of time and longevity, why is a twenty-fifth or fiftieth wedding anniversary so important? What about Valentine's Day, which we have come to celebrate by rote? How can we create closure at the end of an era in our lives, after a divorce or a rupture with a close friend? What can we do to better understand and celebrate meaningful rites of passage in our human existence?

The answers come when we search for and invigorate these events with meaning, definition, and purpose. When we create our own, individual ceremonies to celebrate the special times in our lives, we not only enjoy them more, but we begin the process of giving birth to a whole new structure of family traditions.

CREATING NEW FAMILY TRADITIONS? WHO'S GOT TIME?

Creating a meaningful ceremony does require willingness, time, and energy—primary elements required to accomplish any goal. But it is quite clear that even with all the technology that has not-so-subtly turned us into an instant society with instantly-met-needs, people have less and less time to do the things they want to do. This book aims to give you the basic knowledge needed to make your own ceremonies come to life. Presented are familiar events that can be deeply transformational with the weight, grace, and grandeur that rituals bring. Each ceremony, culled from multicultural celebration practices, includes background information on each ritual to be performed. I suggest appropriate deities for invocations as well as specific herbs, incenses, oils, candles, and other supplies I feel could be useful for a particular celebration. The rest is up to you. The personal love, care, and attention you bring to the effort are the only other elements needed to insure a positive outcome.

CREATING YOUR CEREMONY

Coming up with the elements that make up a ceremony is fun! Anyone can do it—as long as your desire is strong and comes from a place of love, and that you know the outcome you seek is eminently reachable. Never lose sight of the fact that behind every ceremony should be a tangible purpose and objective.

Even though I provide the ceremony in its entirety and give ideas and examples of how to set up each ritual, these are not rules! Each ceremony should be as individual as the person or persons involved, taking into account their characteristics and temperaments, their needs, and the desired goal. The more you go into the groundwork and preparation for the ceremony, the more successful it will be. For example, I may suggest that you call on Venus, goddess of love, as in the Blissful Matrimony Ceremony. However, if you feel more of an attraction or connection to another deity or traditional religious saint, by all means, follow that feeling. If your religion doesn't allow for prayer or communication with deities from other cultures, that's okay. Go with what is familiar and comfortable for you. Same goes for oils, herbs, and incenses. If there is an herb, plant, or flower not mentioned here but which holds special significance for you (the host or subject of the ceremony), feel free to include it. The more personalized, the better. You can read the entire ceremony out loud, directly from this book, filling in the blanks, where indicated. Or you may want to add your own comments, change my words around, or simply use the ceremony as a springboard for creating your own. Nothing is disallowed, as long as it feels right.

PRACTICAL CONSIDERATIONS

If you do decide to use the ceremony as written, please do yourself a favor and read through the entire ceremony before performing it. You may even want to practice reading it out loud in front of a mirror. This way you will quickly figure out where and when you would like to make changes, if any. You can also use this time to practice looking up every once in a while, as you read, to make eye contact with the ceremony's participants. This should not be a lecture, but a process in which everyone feels involved. You will note that throughout I have included bits of humor, in order to keep things light. My humor may not work for you. I only put those asides in there to encourage you to throw in your own comments or remarks, when appropriate. There's nothing like an amusing anecdote to liven things up, make people smile or laugh, and, well, just shake things up a bit. Also, the ceremonies are written for specific events in our lives. But the way we live our lives today definitely does not mirror the lives our parents lived. So keep in mind that although there is a ceremony for healing the pain of divorce, with a little tweaking, this same ceremony can be used for breakups or separations of any nature. Same goes for the Blissful Matrimony Ceremony, which though written in heterosexual-speak, can easily accommodate same-sex couples. In addition, this particular ceremony was conceived for the occasion of a marriage. But it can also be used for all kinds of commitment choices and situations. The ceremony for making peace with death provides many rituals that can be used for other ceremonies of your own making. I can think of plenty of life situations that involve endings and new beginnings—new city, new career, new era. Taken apart, each ceremony offers multiple mini-rituals for whatever life throws your way. Use them!

CREATING A SPECIAL ENVIRONMENT

We bring sacred space into being when we gather together. When considering the look you want to give the space or room in which you plan to hold your ceremony, you may want to go all out. Draping beautiful fabric along your mantelpiece, replacing existing paintings or photographs on the wall with an appropriate wall hanging borrowed from a friend, or draping dark fabric along windows to dim the room are great ideas. Or you might prefer your room exactly as it is, sunlight streaming in and all! If you don't want to make an altar, you can use your mantelpiece, as I once did. I placed on it all the ceremonial accoutrements, such as candles and incense, and made that spot the focal point for each ritual. The more you do to make the space feel divine, the better. Keep in mind that you don't have to incur great expense to transform a space. Knowing that I love scarves, shawls, and beautiful fabrics, a friend of mine recently stopped by to survey my cache. She wanted to work within a certain color scheme for her ceremony, and she knew I would be able to lend her something fabulous and glittery in pastel pink for her New Baby Ceremony. If this all feels like redecorating or designing and you don't feel so disposed, engage a friend or even the subject of the ceremony, who may thoroughly enjoy helping you with the preparations.

WHAT SHOULD I WEAR?

There are no dos and don'ts. You may feel like getting into priestess mode just for the fun of it. This does not mean you have to wear long, flowing robes. Whatever your mood, wear something that makes you feel radiant and comfortable with your appearance. You could wrap a simple sarong around your waist and go barefoot, or wear a long skirt with a loose top. Wrapping a scarf around your head may add a touch of drama. Of course, if you often wear scarves, then go with a bare head just for effect. Maybe this is the time to wear those large-beaded necklaces and hoop earrings you have stuffed in a drawer somewhere—jewelry can certainly add special energy to your person. Feel free to adorn and decorate your body! On the other hand, depending on the intended guests, you may prefer to present yourself exactly as you always do, just to make people more comfortable.

WHERE DO I FIND ALL THE STUFF FOR MY CEREMONY?

Most of the supplies I recommend you use to create your ceremony should be easy to find. Your own kitchen cabinet may very well turn out to be a treasure chest when it comes to herbs, unless you are not much of a cook. In that case, your local supermarket should do the trick. With the popularity of aromatherapy, finding essential oils is as easy as going down to the corner health-food store. Candles, in a plethora of colors, are now available everywhere! Sage sticks, charcoal blocks, incense, bells, and crystals are all fairly inexpensive items, and can be found in any New Age store. If there are no New Age-type stores in your area, I recommend you hop on the Internet for a quick search. In many cases, you will be able to order the things you need online. For the more obscure herbs and oils, check the bibliography of this book. Many of the books referenced offer resource sections, where you can mail order most of the items mentioned.

Of course, you can always consider substituting a suggested herb or oil for another. There are many books on the market that detail the magical properties of herbs, flowers, plants, and trees. In that regard, in order to avoid potential confusion, I want to clarify one point: throughout the book I describe characteristics and attributes of various elements, such as colors, flowers, stones, herbs, etc. Please keep in mind that, in many cases, those attributes are numerous and varied. I did not think it would be necessary to mention them all, only the ones appropriate to the ritual at hand. For example, the color red is associated with success, passion and vitality. I may mention only success in one ritual and only passion in another.

INVITATION

A friend of mine recently sent out a typical wedding shower invitation, only there was an added line:

"Ceremony begins at 6:00 P.M. Sharp!"

No one knew quite what to make of it, but they were all intrigued and excited. You may want to make it a formal invitation to a ceremony or simply an invitation to a party "with a special event to begin at _____." It's up to you. Perhaps this is the perfect time to use a blank invitation card with your own handwritten or printed words inside. Be creative!

DEALING WITH THAT
ANTI-NEW-AGE BIAS

Explaining why a certain ritual is done helps take the mystery out of it. That's why I include brief informative and historical introductions to each ritual before they are to be performed. Read them as worded or reword them, add to them, feel free to make them yours. Sharing information with participants during a ceremony is a wonderful way to maintain everyone's attention and to keep them involved. A little knowledge goes a long way in appeasing the cynics in the crowd.

The most important thing to remember when preparing for a ceremony is intent. The next most important thing is fun! Though it does require thoughtfulness, and the wonderful quiet of concentration, by all means keep it light. Ceremonies are not meant to be solemn, boring affairs. They are participatory events where everyone is encouraged to share as much of their energy as possible. So, enjoy!

EVERYDAY CELEBRATIONS

HEART & HOME

Creating a Dwelling Divine

INTRODUCTION

It doesn't need to be a new, recently purchased house or apartment for it to warrant a home blessing ceremony. However, just before moving into your new place is an ideal time to bless your new home. It is usually free of its last occupants' belongings, so it is also the perfect time to imprint it with your own energy and intention. But even if you are moving into a furnished place or moving in as a new roommate, you can still bless your home with a ceremony. If your new roommate is not open to it, you can do your ceremony in the parts of the home that are designated as yours. That, of course, is for your housemate and you to discuss. My husband is open to space clearing but the last time I wanted to do a ceremony, I could not pin him down on a day and time to do it. So I finally did it on my own one evening, when I knew he would be gone for a few hours. I had the house all to myself—a rare treat—and I thoroughly enjoyed the process. He was not aware of my activities but as soon as he walked in the door, he exclaimed, "Wow, the house feels great! What did you do?"

We have owned an art gallery for a number of years, and send out invitations to exhibits and events at least four or five times a year. It never ceases to amaze me how often people move. This is why I know there is a need for creating rituals around a new environment destined to be home. Sometimes a new living situation is considered "only temporary" so people put off making it "their own." You can forever delay displaying cherished photographs and artwork or buying plants and knickknacks because you think you won't be there long. But that would be a mistake. Temporary can become long-term before you know it. Time has that way about it. And living out of a suitcase and boxes can quickly become depressing. I encourage infusing your place with as many personal touches as possible so that you can continue enjoying your days right now as the gifts that they are from the universe.

Performing a ceremony is a wonderful way to begin making a place yours. Now, you might be one of those rare people who have lived in the same place for years. You may love your place, have no reason to move, but you just ended a relationship and want to clear the space of that person's vibrations. Or perhaps you've just done some much-needed spring cleaning and feel the need to rejuvenate the energy of your home. Maybe you threw a big party and there was a lot of smoking, or perhaps some of the guests were not welcome. No matter the reason—whether to clean up, shake things up, open up to new possibilities, or close yourself off from unwanted energies—a home-blessing ceremony makes it easier for you to connect with your space and to help transform it into your special sanctuary.

Home. Barring unusual circumstances, that word conjures up warm, fuzzy feelings and emotions. Home is the place you hurry to after a long day's work, the place you can't wait to see again after a long trip. You want to sleep in your own bed and eat a home-cooked meal. Home is the place where you feel comfortable, where you can put your feet up and relax, where lounging around in pajamas feels great. In putting together this ceremony, I wanted to focus on all of those elements that define what people seek and expect from "home"—being home, making a home, hearth and home, finding that place called home. To that end, it can safely be said that people look to their home for:

Refuge
Shelter
Comfort
Warmth
Rest
Peace
Harmony
Safety
A space for contemplation
A joyful and loving environment

The following ceremony can be done alone* or with the help of friends whose loving and supportive energy you would find helpful in your home. As always, feel free to improvise on my suggestions. Do improve upon, add to, delete from, and personalize as much as possible. This is your home!

---

* If you are doing this alone, there is no need to read instructions out loud; simply follow directions and perform actions.

PRE-CEREMONY PREPARATIONS

Before performing a home-blessing ceremony, it is always recommended that you go through your place and throw out or give away old stuff (clothes, food, dust collectors, unusable or unused equipment, appliances, etc.). If you cannot, your ceremony will still work because intention is everything. However, it probably won't be quite as effective. Clearing out the old to make room for the new is an old adage that, whether we like it or not, makes a lot of sense. I read somewhere long ago that we are linked to all our possessions by invisible, cobweb-like filaments that supposedly run from our fingertips to each item we own. If you think about it, that means there are probably hundreds of these threads attached to our bodies. This is probably why we occasionally feel the need to clean out our closets and pantries, have a garage sale, and give things away. They are weighing us down! And this is why spring cleaning feels so good. We feel so much lighter, so much freer, and so satisfied! If you can't have a major spring-cleaning session, do the best you can. The more you clear out before your ceremony, the more dramatic will be your results.

In order to perform this ceremony, you will need the following items:

- Broom and/or vacuum
- Mop and/or sponge
- Small bowl, dinner-sized plate, three candleholders
- Candles (one brown, one white and two red)
- Cumin seeds
- Handful of dirt
- Matches
- Lavender essential oil
- Peppermint essential oil
- Fresh red rose petals
- Fresh sprig of rosemary (if possible) or dried rosemary
- Sage stick
- Rock or sea salt
- Spray bottle
- Spring water

(CONTINUED)

Symbolic pictures and/or objects that demonstrate a feeling or quality you might want in the different rooms of your home, such as:

෨ Small branch from a tree

෨ A bunch of violets or a gardenia

෨ Your favorite fruit(s) and/or vegetable(s) to represent the nourishment (of body and soul) that takes place in your kitchen and dining room

෨ For the bedroom, place a cup of chamomile tea (for restful sleep) next to a chunk of chocolate (for its aphrodisiac and lustful properties) on a cutout of a paper heart (for love)

෨ Photograph(s) of a loving moment between you and your mate or friend(s) to represent the overall love element

෨ Photograph or image from a book or magazine of a waterfall to represent your bathroom and the cleansing (of body and soul) that you want to enjoy there

෨ A photograph or a page from a magazine of an ideal and harmonious setting (indoor or outdoor) to represent harmony in your living room

You can also gather beloved items with special significance, such as a special book or paragraph from a book, a cherished poem, love letters, favorite cards, deity representations either in statuary or photo format, etc. as long as they represent a feeling you want in your home. Be selective, but by all means include what's important to you.

All above items are to be placed in an eye-pleasing arrangement on a dedicated altar space when indicated. And keep in mind, you will need time and energy—a home-blessing ceremony can take time, depending on the size of your home and it involves some physical labor.

REMINDER: *Please remember to read through the ceremony in its entirety so that you can make appropriate changes. Practice reading it out loud in order to familiarize yourself and become comfortable with it. Most importantly, if the way I have written it does not feel suitable for you, or in keeping with the way you would normally express yourself, simply use it as a guideline for your own words where needed.*

PLEASE NOTE: *All sections of the ceremony are meant to be read out loud, except for instructions set in italics.*

HEART AND HOME
Creating a Dwelling Divine

WELCOME

Welcome, everyone. The ceremony we are about to partake in has been conceived with love, and it is assumed that everyone here has come to bring wishes of love and well-being to _____ [person who lives there] and to her/his home.

CEREMONY

We will begin with sweeping, which helps to usher out old, stale energy.

Sweep out your place or, if you have carpeting, use a vacuum cleaner.

SMUDGE WITH SAGE

Smudging purifies with the smoke of sage branches bound together into a stick. According to Native American beliefs, smudging removes negative energy and remnants of negative energy from people, places, and things.

Using a match, light your sage stick*. Once it starts to burn, blow it out. There should be plenty of smoke pouring from it. Start by smudging yourself first. Wave the sage stick up, down, and all around yourself while asking all worries, stresses, and concerns to go away and leave you alone. If there are other participants, smudge each person in turn. Walk the perimeter of

* If sage stick is not available, substitute with sage incense stick.

your home, going in and out of each room while fanning the smoke up and down into all corners, angles and toward the ceilings. If your place is furnished, wave the sage stick around each piece of furniture, if you like. As you do this, remember that what you think about, you attract. So think about or envision your home filled with a bright white light edging out all dark and negative feelings and forces. When you have completed this process, open all windows and doors for a few minutes in order to offer a point of exit to any negative energy. If there are many participants, you might ask different people to smudge different rooms.

PURIFY

It is a widely held belief throughout many civilizations that salt is an agent for cleansing and purification. Peppermint purifies by elevating the vibration of an area.

Fill a bucket with spring water and dissolve three tablespoons of sea salt or rock salt into it. If possible, use seawater instead. Add four drops of peppermint essential oil and mix. If you have hardwood, tile, or linoleum floors, using a new or clean mop, wash with this mixture. Also, using a clean sponge or cloth, rub mixture on furniture, doors, and walls as best you can. If you have carpeting, skip this step.

Once this is done, place a pinch of salt on your front doorstep *[to ensure safety]* and in corners to lift any remaining impurities. After the ceremony, or the following day, vacuum these away or lift with a sponge and flush down the toilet.

CREATE AN ALTAR

An altar is traditionally considered a special place where human beings can meet with God, the divine, that Great Mystery, or whatever term you use for the sacred. It is a place to make offerings to deities whose favors and help you want to formally request. It is also an area designated to reflect the element and intent of any given ceremony.

Choose the main room in your home or the room in which you plan to spend the most time. Designate a table or a spot on the floor as your altar. As you place the items suggested below on the altar, remember that with these offerings to the gods, goddesses, elemental spirits, and to Mother Nature you are indicating your desires to the universe. Take your time, make the prettiest arrangement possible, and lovingly create the way you would like to live, feel, and experience your home. In all cases, if there are many present, simply read the instructions and explanations out loud.

Place on the altar your photographs and other appropriate objects and imagery, as suggested in the Pre-Ceremony Preparations list above. As you do this, take the time to experience the feeling represented in each photo or object coming to life in each room.

Fill a plate with freshly picked red rose petals, which serve to generate warm, joyful, abundant vibrations in the home. Place a white candle in the center to invite clarity, spiritual guidance, and the brilliant light of God into your household. Set it on the altar in a spot of your choice and light the candle.

On separate individual plates or in individual candleholders, place a brown candle to represent and invite the spirit of Mother Earth. As you light the candle, say:

Mother Earth, you are the first real property-owner, please ground and stabilize me and my living situation. Please bless this home with your presence and goodness.

A red candle to represent and invite Bosou, Haitian protector spirit. As you light the candle, say:

Dear Haitian protector spirit, Bosou, your image as a fertile bull is with me as I ask you to impart to me the earth's gifts and to bless this home so that no harm might come to it or me when I am in it.

Another red candle to represent Roman god Janus. As you light the candle, say:

Dear Roman god Janus, master of gates and doorways, who opens the path to opportunity. Please fill this home with good fortune.

To deter burglars and thieves, scatter a handful of cumin seeds on the altar.

To prevent fire, place a handful of dirt in a bowl, add spring water and mix with a wooden stick or small branch from a tree to represent the earth's ability to absorb fire and water's ability to put it out. Once mixed, place it alongside the other items on the altar.

Place a bunch of violets or a gardenia on the altar for the element of peace.

Fill your spray bottle with spring water, add four drops of lavender essential oil and shake. Place it on the altar.

Once you have made your offerings, sit back, close your eyes, and speak, whisper, or make a silent prayer of thanks for the gifts you are about to receive or have, in fact, already received!

Finally, to complete your ceremony, lift the spray bottle from the altar and walk around each room of your home. As you do so, spray a fine mist to fill the air with the clean, fresh scent of lavender and its peaceful, restful, loving, and healing properties.

Extinguish all candles before going to sleep, but feel free to relight them every day henceforth until they burn down. You may leave the altar as it is until you feel the time is right to take it apart. Or you may want to break it down the same or next day— you will know exactly when to do it.

END OF CEREMONY

ANNIVERSARY
Renewing Bonds, Reviewing Promises

INTRODUCTION

When you stop to think about what it takes before two people find each other and then proceed to create a life together, it's a wonder it ever happens at all. First there has to be chemistry, then you have to like the way he looks, and he has to somehow fit your idea of the right mate. These considerations include earning power (whatever level that is for you), values, spiritual or religious considerations, family approval, and whether he wants a family with you or not. Then there are the lifestyle issues: vegetarian vs. meat eating; socially oriented or homebody; cynical outlook vs. cheery disposition? Outdoor sports-type or only at the gym? And what about spending patterns? Expensive cars vs. travel? In addition to all this, you have to enjoy each other in bed! Bottom line, are you compatible? In light of the endless potential potholes and wrong turns a couple can take, in the game of love anniversaries are a triumph, and the participants nothing less than heroes!

Now don't get me wrong. In case you're thinking I sound battle-scarred, I love being married and this year will celebrate my fifteenth wedding anniversary. Our years of marriage have not been marked by any major crisis; we love each other, are good friends, and enjoy each other's company. We travel well together, we have many of the same goals, and emotionally we support each other better than most. It's just that day-to-day life with another person is challenging, to put it mildly. Putting it bluntly, it's work. So I see anniversaries as an opportunity to pat ourselves on the back for work well done. It's a time to release some of those niggling hurts and disappointments we tend to hold onto, and to appreciate the wonderful moments we enjoyed together the year before. It's a time to make promises again; getting it right isn't always easy, but intention counts a lot! Celebrate the choice you made to be together. Reflect on the roads traveled together and re-evaluate planned destinations. Recommit to each other in ways that count—you know each other better now and thus know exactly what your partner needs. Make a list of your new ambitions toward each other, write them down and invite your friends to be eyewitnesses.

Staying together requires love, willingness to make that a priority, support from your friends and family, and giving yourself that occasional pat on the back. This Anniversary Ceremony aims to help us do that.

Unless the anniversary is a major one and offspring are involved in helping to plan it, usually it is the couple that decides to throw a party to celebrate it. This ceremony is written in first-person format and is intended to be performed at a gathering attended by friends and family. You can make it a focus of your party, or if you prefer to perform it together, just the two of you, I provide suggestions on ways to alter the rituals for that situation. If someone else is hosting it, just change the pronouns to the third person or the couple's names, where appropriate. Of course, each marriage or meaningful relationship is different and comes with its own set of issues. I have attempted to keep things general by staying with safe, common-to-all, relationship issues, like communication and compromise, etc. It is imperative that you inject into it as much of yourself and your personal issues as possible so that this ceremony works for you.

And another thing . . . Every time I visualized the rituals for this ceremony, I would inject my husband and myself to gauge whether this would be something we might actually do. Mushy, public, and poetic declarations of love and commitment just didn't feel right. The ceremony is meant to replace the quick toast of champagne, evening out, and gift exchange, but I want it to be lighthearted and fun as well as serious, and certainly not corny. I hope I've achieved my goal. However, if you feel absolutely in your element with effusive displays of affection, by all means, express yourself! Please change my words to fit your life.

I have also included suggested variations for the BIG anniversaries—the first, fifth, tenth, twenty-fifth, and fiftieth—based on simple numerological principles (please see Numerology section in body of ceremony). Please use the appropriate one as befits the anniversary year in question.

PRE-CEREMONY PREPARATIONS

Before the day of the ceremony, take time with your husband (or mate) to prepare a list of five to ten vows and resolutions you promise to keep for that year in order to make your relationship the best it can be. The first three vows on your list should be the top three things your husband would like to see you do. Write them down on your list in the first person, and then finish your list. Your husband's list should begin with your top three wishes, written in the first person. These can include day-to-day things like "I promise to put my dirty socks in the hamper instead of on the hamper." Type up each list on a letter-size sheet of paper, with a signature line just under the last wish. Leave plenty of room at the bottom for your guests to fill these sheets with their signatures as eyewitnesses to your resolutions.

Each prepare another list of five to ten things (or more) you are thankful for in your relationship. These should be general things like "thank you for rubbing my back when it aches" as well as more specific things that were great about the last year together—special moments, thoughtful words or acts, something fun you did together.

Prepare an altar or table. Place whatever items on it that you think are reflective of your union or of love in general. These can include:

- Hearts of any kind, i.e., chocolate hearts and any heart-shaped objects

- Photo of the two of you (this can be a wedding photo or another photo that is special to you)

- Rose incense stick (light before beginning of ceremony)

- Other items special to you both

(CONTINUED)

Other items needed (these can be placed on altar or nearby for easy access):

🕯 One bell

🕯 Two candles (larger, pillar type)—one light blue (to represent him) and one light green (to represent you)

🕯 Matches

🕯 Pens

🕯 Pitcher filled with spring water

🕯 One rosebush plant (this can be a young rosebush, just planted, or a blooming one–that's up to you; size of plant is also at your discretion)

🕯 Copies of runic table (available on page 186 in this book). Make as many copies as there will be participants or guests, including yourself

🕯 Toothpicks

🕯 Vase with one red rose, or red and pink roses

REMINDER: *Please remember to read through the ceremony in its entirety so that you can make appropriate changes. Practice reading it out loud in order to familiarize yourself and become comfortable with it. Most importantly, if the way I have written it does not feel suitable for you, or in keeping with the way you would normally express yourself, simply use it as a guideline for your own words where needed. This ceremony is written in heterosexual language. If the couple in question is same-sex, simply change the terms "husband" or "spouse" to "partner" or "mate."*

PLEASE NOTE: All sections of the ceremony are meant to be read out loud, except for instructions set in italics.

ANNIVERSARY
Renewing Bonds, Reviewing Promises

WELCOME

Welcome, everyone. The ceremony we are about to partake in has been conceived with love, and it is assumed that everyone here has come to bring wishes of love and well-being to _____ *[mate]* and me in honor of our anniversary.

CEREMONY

The stringing together of certain rituals performed with special intent is called ceremony. Ceremonies are important because they serve to gather up all of our energies and to focus them on one specific thing: in this case, helping _____ *[mate]* and I to take a look at each other with new eyes as we celebrate our wedding anniversary. Hopefully you won't think us self-indulgent. People's intentions count. And if you are here, rooting for us to enjoy each other for a long, long time, then I believe we will! (Call me silly!)

Choosing a predetermined time, place, and setting for an event; using symbolic words, aromas, sounds, and actions; and adding the participation of special people, all have the effect of lifting us out of our everyday frame of reference into the realm of the extraordinary, where anything and everything is possible simply because we wish it to be. Although some of the rituals we do today might seem strange, they have all been carefully researched in the hope of recreating centuries-old practices from various corners of the world. These rituals serve to harness the positive power of the saints, spirits, angels, gods, and goddesses that surround us, and to make our desires known to them. As you know, if you don't ask, you won't receive.

BELL

I am going to start by ringing this bell around the perimeter of the room. Three thousand years ago, in recognizing that everything in creation was imbued with a life force or energy, the ancient Chinese started practicing Feng Shui *[pronounced Feng Shway]* as a practical means of redirecting the flow of energy in a space. It created powerful adjustments that efficiently changed the course of their lives. Today Feng Shui is widely accepted as a natural way to attune oneself with the elements. This helps to harmonize, balance, and enhance the flow and level of energy in one's environment. The use of bells is prevalent in Feng Shui practices primarily to purify a space, disperse static energy, and to create a sacred circle of sound. This vibration and movement serves to ward off negative spirits and to attract the angels. We use the bell here today for the same purpose. Please listen to its tone. Clear your mind of any concerns and let it fill your being as you allow your energy to vibrate at a new, heightened level.

So, anniversaries. Why are they important to celebrate? It's so easy to go out to dinner, toast each other with champagne, and have a party without ever really giving much thought to the reason behind the festivities. And when you think about how unlikely it is that two people should meet and have enough of the tumblers fall into place for them to go on a second date, that's cause for celebration enough! All those elements—chemistry, timing, openness, acceptance of each others' quirks, the financials, peer and parental acceptance, compatibility, not to mention all that day-to-day stuff—the mere fact that they all come together to the point where you're celebrating an anniversary is downright life affirming. So gratitude, or just not taking a long-term relationship for granted, is worthy of our consideration. An anniversary also gives us an opportunity to begin again—not necessarily the relationship in its entirety, but just one year at a time. It is a perfect time to remember the year gone by, just to single out the good times, and to let go of the difficult ones. Why wait for the New Year to make resolutions, when an anniversary is so appropriate? We know best the things that work and the things that don't. Making new promises to fulfill each other's hopes is not a bad idea. I think lists are in order! But I'll get to that later. An anniversary is worth celebrating for the friendship and partnership that comes with it. And, as anyone who's ever been in one knows, relationships take work, so it is also a time to reward ourselves for work well done. A union between two people involves commitment; it involves a willingness to look at things from the other person's perspective and agreement on a destination, as well as how to get there. And most of all, a long-term relationship takes love, the power that binds the two of us together, the force that connects us all to one another, and the most important thing we celebrate tonight.

So the first thing I am going to do is to invite some potent love energies to join us tonight in order to set the mood.

INVOCATION

I call upon the spirit of Cupid; Roman love goddess, Venus, Greek love goddess, Aphrodite; and Haitian love goddess, Erzulie. Please bless this ceremony with your powers of love. Help everyone in this room tap into the love in their hearts so that all of our rituals might come to fruition. Thank you.

If the anniversary in question is one of the major anniversaries—first, fifth, tenth, twentieth, twenty-fifth, or fiftieth-- read appropriate paragraph below. If your ceremony is not for one of the special anniversaries, please skip down to the paragraph following the fiftieth wedding anniversary paragraph.

NUMEROLOGY

Tonight we celebrate our _____ *[anniversary year]* anniversary. Numerology speaks to the symbolism around numbers and is typically used to determine the personality or characteristics of a person based on her year of birth. That number is arrived at by adding up all of the digits in the day, month, and year of that person's birthday. The digits that make up the number resulting from that equation are further added together until it is reduced down to one digit. For example, for a person born on January 1, 1965, you would add together 1 + 1 + 1 + 9 + 6 + 5, which equals 23. When you add 2 + 3, you get the number 5. Everything in the world resonates at a specific frequency, and numbers are no different. The basic symbolism of numbers 1 through 9 is generally accepted in the field of numerology. In this particular instance, we use these simple, basic symbols to arrive at the vibration, which surrounds the personality, not of _____ [mate] or me, but of our anniversary year. In this case the number _____ [number of years married]. This number represents the influences that we will be working with this year. It is also a foreshadowing of possible opportunities waiting to make themselves available to us.

Choose appropriate anniversary and read one of the following paragraphs out loud.

FIRST ANNIVERSARY

The energy around the number 1 is of independence, individuality, creativity, originality, and leadership. The other side of the number 1 is ego, or being full of it. This information makes it easy to see why the first year of any marriage is so crucial. While we yearn to bind ourselves to each other, we also seek to retain our wholeness. These are good tendencies, if we choose to make them so. So, with that in mind, what I have here is a planted rosebush, which represents our relationship.

FIFTH ANNIVERSARY

The energy around the number 5 is one of excitement, variety, and progressive thinking. Productive and positive use of freedom is explored, and adaptability comes with ease. The other side of the number 5 is a tendency toward inconsistency and excess in the realm of the senses. So, with that in mind, what I have here is a planted rosebush, which represents our relationship.

TENTH ANNIVERSARY

When 1 and 0 are added together, you get the number 1. The energy around the number 1 is of independence, individuality, creativity, originality, and leadership. The other side of the number 1 is ego, or being full of it. When you think about it, the inclinations for the first and tenth year of marriage are the same. These tendencies not only speak to this coming year, but to the next decade as well! Like life, everything works in cycles that come back around to show us what we've learned or need to learn. So, with that in mind, what I have here is a planted rosebush, which represents our relationship.

TWENTIETH ANNIVERSARY

When 2 and 0 are added together, you get the number 2. The energy around the number 2 is one of harmony, consideration, closeness, thoughtfulness, and stability. The other side of number 2 is a tendency toward oversensitivity and neediness. When you think about it, the inclinations for the second and twentieth year of marriage are the same. These tendencies not only speak to this coming year but to the next two decades, as well! Like life, everything works in cycles that come back around to show us what we've learned or need to learn. So, with that in mind, what I have here is a planted rosebush, which represents our relationship.

TWENTY-FIFTH ANNIVERSARY

When 2 and 5 are added together, you get the number 7. The energy around the number 7 is one of spirituality, wisdom, analysis, and introspection. The other side of the number 7 is a tendency toward blame and suppression of feelings. We have plenty to look forward to and plenty to look out for! So, with that in mind, what I have here is a planted rosebush, which represents our relationship.

FIFTIETH ANNIVERSARY

When 5 and 0 are added together, you get the number 5. The energy around the number 5 is one of excitement, variety, and progressive thinking. Productive and positive use of freedom is explored, and adaptability comes with ease. The other side of the number 5 is a tendency toward inconsistency and excess in the realm of the senses. When you think about it, the inclinations for the fifth and fiftieth year of marriage are the same. These tendencies not only speak to this coming year, but to the next fifty years, as well! Like life, everything works in cycles that come back around to show us what we've learned or need to learn. So, with that in mind, what I have here is a planted rosebush, which represents our relationship.

HERBS, FLOWERS, PLANTS, AND TREES

The gifts that Mother Nature has bestowed upon us—her flowers, plants, trees and herbs—are there to remind us of our connection to the earth. The life force that exists in human beings brings us the magic of breath. The life force within green, growing things also serves to nourish, revitalize, heal, and intoxicate us while bringing home our interdependent nature with Mother Earth. Endless numbers of books have been written on the medicinal and magical properties of herbs, flowers, plants, and trees. We use this rosebush tonight, fully thankful for her wonderful attributes and for her power to bring her special gifts into our lives.

Roses have long been associated with love. Roses are believed to carry powerful love magic and are used to attract love. When rose water is added to bathwater, it becomes a love bath; and rose hips (the fruit of the rose), when strung and worn as beads, are considered love magnets. It is said that the elements of earth, fire, air, and water exist in all living things in varying amounts, and that each element is associated with certain magical properties. The ruling element of the rose is water, whose magical uses include love, friendship, and fidelity.

I ask you to imagine that this rosebush represents our relationship. I'm going to come around the room with it and with this pitcher of spring water. Please water the plant, and by association, our relationship, with just a few drops of this magical water (we don't want to drown it!). This symbolizes your intention that our marriage *[or union]* be blessed with long-lasting love, friendship, and fidelity!

If this is a large gathering, it may make more sense to have everyone come to where the plant is to take a turn at watering it. This may also be the case if you prefer to use a larger plant. Start by watering the plant yourself, and then hold it out to your mate, who should do the same. Then go around the room or invite people to come up to the plant's location. But before you do, read the following out loud.

While I go around the room, just to keep things in the right mood, I suggest the rest of you tell each other love stories. You can talk about your favorite romantic movie, book, or personal story—first time you fell in love, etc.

When everyone has had a turn, ring the bell to signal the end of this ritual.

Thanks, everyone; that was great. But we're just getting warmed up! Here's what we're going to do next. I have two candles here, and several copies of a runic table. The blue candle represents _____ *[mate]* and the green one represents me.

CANDLES

The practice of candle burning is rooted in our primitive ancestors' belief in the power of fire to bring us closer to the light, to help us attain enlightenment, and to prepare our environment for the gifts of the divine. The tradition of burning birthday candles comes from the belief that they carry our wishes up to God, the higher self, or that Great Mystery, depending on how you feel about that term.

RUNES

Runes are the alphabet of the ancient Scandinavian peoples, and each symbol has a generally accepted magical meaning attached to it. Please take a copy of the runic table, study it for a moment, and then choose the runic symbol that most closely represents the wish, desire, or goal you want to see manifested for _____ [mate] and for me as a result of this ceremony. Then take a toothpick and use it to inscribe or scratch that symbol into each candle. Basically, give us whatever you think we need! As you do this, remember to ask the Highest to help make this wish a reality.

I'm going to go first, then _____ [mate], then I ask you to come up, one at a time. Again, while we take the time to do this, more love stories!

When everyone has had a turn, ring bell to get everyone's attention. Light your candle, have your mate light his. Ring bell to signal the end of this ritual. Read the following out loud.

Thank you all so much. The last thing we're going to do brings us back to that list I mentioned earlier. _____ [mate] and I have each prepared two lists. One lists the things in our relationship for which we are thankful; and the other is a list of vows, resolutions, and promises we've made to each other for this next year. The top three promises on my list are the things _____ [mate] wishes I would do, but they're down on paper as if I'd written them. And the same goes for his top three. We are going to make the bold move of reading them out loud to each other and to you, then we ask you to sign each of our lists of promises as eyewitnesses! In the coming year, we ask for your support, encouragement, and especially your REMINDERS, in case we forget, that we promised to do these things in the hope of making our relationship the best it can be. With your help, good intentions, and loving energy, we both feel we can only get better!

But before we read these, I want to say to my husband *[turn to husband]*:

I love you and respect you and thank you for being my friend. I want to thank you for helping me to be the best I can be, and I look forward to spending the rest of my life with you.

Of course, the above is just a suggestion. You and your spouse should put this into your own words ahead of time. If you decide to use these words, feel free to add to or delete from it as necessary.

After you finish reading your statement, have your husband read the same statement back to you. Hug and kiss, or whatever the spirit moves you to do.

Read your list of promises out loud, and then sign at the bottom. Invite your mate to read his out loud, and then have him sign it. Have champagne or favorite libation ready for a toast. Read the following out loud.

Before you come up to sign this important document, which you can do at your own pace throughout the evening, we'd like to propose a toast to love, to our marriage and to you, our friends, for making this the best anniversary party we've ever had!

Perfect music to play at this time would be your wedding song or song special to you both.

END OF CEREMONY

HAPPY BIRTHDAY

Thanksgiving for Life

INTRODUCTION

I grew up in a family that made a big deal over birthdays. Maybe I would get to have a party, maybe not, but between my parents, sisters and brother, friends, godparents, and grandparents, I always received lots of presents. I got to choose what everyone watched on television that night, we always had cake, and I was treated like royalty. Then, around age twenty-two, I moved away from my family to another state where I knew only one or two people. That year when my birthday rolled around, I awoke when the phone rang. It was my mother and father calling to wish me a happy birthday. That call was followed by a quick burst of other calls from my sisters and brother. I got dressed and went to work where my two workmates were thoughtful enough to offer token gifts and that was the end of that. No one else knew or remembered it was my birthday, there was no cake and candles, and I was too tight for cash to treat myself to something special. I went home and impatiently waited for the day to end.

For the last twelve years, I have been married to a man who loves me very much, but in his family, birthday rituals were next to none. He doesn't understand when I get upset that he forgets or doesn't make a fuss. I gather from friends that mine is not an uncommon experience, which leads me to think that we need to rethink birthdays. Whether a birthday is happy or not tends to depend on who remembers or doesn't. But birthdays are so much more than that! We've reduced them to gifts, birthday cakes, and parties, not even stopping to remember what it is we so itch to celebrate. And there is cause for celebration! If no one else remembers, it's okay, because I guarantee you that whether you do a ceremony around your birthday with fifty people or just by yourself, you will feel richer, more thankful, and filled with love for all the goodness in your life.

Birthdays are a great time to take stock, to get rid of old notions and concepts about who you are. You get the chance to be born again, to indulge in the wondrousness of the five senses you were given, and to honor your body and the woman whose body you came through. Birth is the polar opposite of death. Acknowledge your aliveness and your ability to create the life you want for yourself.

The following ceremony is written so that it can be performed with many friends as part of, or instead of, the typical birthday party. However, it can also be done by one's self. Rather than reading the individual ritual introductions out loud, simply read them to yourself, and then perform the ritual. Where necessary, I give indications on how to proceed if the ceremony is being performed solo. Either way, it will be immensely gratifying. Also, it is perfectly okay to host or initiate a ceremony for yourself. You need only replace the third person pronouns with the words "I" or "me."

I have also included suggested variations for the BIG birthdays—the sixteenth, twenty-first, thirtieth, fortieth, and fiftieth—based on simple numerological principles (please see numerology section in body of ceremony for additional information on the science of numerology). Please use the appropriate one as befits the birthday year in question.

PRE-CEREMONY PREPARATIONS

Pick a spot and create an altar (choose a table, mantel, or spot on the floor). Feel free to place items that reflect Birthday Girl (baby photo or current photo or other items you associate with her, or that she likes). All of the items listed items can also be placed on or near the altar, whichever you prefer. Items needed:

- One bell

- Single-stem flowers, as many as there are participants in ceremony

- One platter, on which single flowers should be placed

- One empty platter on which participants will place their flower offerings

- One white candle to be placed in center of empty flower platter (burn bottom of candle until wax drips onto platter, then set candle down)

- Paper cut in small strips, on which people will write the element that they feel birthday girl needs to let go of

- Pens or pencils—as many as there are participants

- Bowl, in which to place all folded strips of paper

- Heat-resistant container, in which to burn strips of paper
  (if fireplace is not available)

- Matches

- One plastic baggie

- Essential oils: almond, eucalyptus, gardenia, and lavender
  Fill one of the pitchers with water, add two to three drops of each oil,
  and mix prior to ceremony

- Two pitchers

- Spring water

- One plant, any size you like

- Birthday cake, birthday candles

- One sage smudge stick or sage incense

REMINDER: *Please remember to read through the ceremony in its entirety so that you can make appropriate changes. Practice reading it out loud in order to familiarize yourself and become comfortable with it. Most importantly, if the way I have written it does not feel suitable for you, or in keeping with the way you would normally express yourself, simply use it as a guideline for your own words where needed.*

PLEASE NOTE: All sections of the ceremony are meant to be read out loud, except for instructions set in italics.

HAPPY BIRTHDAY
Thanksgiving for Life

WELCOME

Welcome, everyone. This ceremony has been conceived with love, and it is assumed that everyone here has come to bring wishes of love and well-being to _____ *[birthday girl]*.

CEREMONY

The stringing together of certain rituals performed with special intent is called ceremony. Ceremonies are important because they serve to gather up all of our energies and to focus them on one specific thing, in this case, helping _____ *[birthday girl]* to celebrate the day she was born, and all that that means. Choosing a predetermined time, place, and setting for an event; using symbolic words, aromas, sounds, and actions; and adding the participation of special people, all has the effect of lifting us out of our everyday frame of reference into the realm of the extraordinary, where anything and everything is possible simply because we wish it to be. Although some of the rituals we do today might seem strange, they have all been carefully researched in the hope of recreating centuries-old practices from various corners of the world. These rituals serve to harness the positive power of the saints, spirits, angels, gods, and goddesses that surround us and to make our desires known to them. As you know, if you don't ask, you won't receive.

BELL

I am going to start the ceremony by ringing this bell around the perimeter of the room. Three thousand years ago, in recognizing that everything in creation was imbued with a life force or energy, the ancient Chinese started practicing Feng Shui *[pronounced Feng Shway]* as a practical means of redirecting the flow of energy in a space. It created powerful adjustments that efficiently changed the course of their life. Today Feng Shui is widely accepted as a natural way to attune oneself with the elements. This helps to harmonize, balance, and enhance the flow and level of energy in one's environment. The use of bells is prevalent in Feng Shui practices primarily to purify a space, disperse static energy, and to create a sacred circle of sound. This vibration and movement serves to ward off negative spirits and to attract the angels. We use the bell here today for the same purpose. Please listen to its tone. Let it fill your being as you allow your energy to vibrate at a new, heightened level.

Walk slowly around perimeter of the room as you ring the bell. Repeat as many times as you wish until you feel a change or clearing of the vibration in the room. Once around the room is usually enough.

We are here to honor _____ *[birthday girl]*, who is celebrating her _____ *[year number, i.e., first, twenty-fifth, etc.]* year of life.

If the birthday in question is one of the major birthdays—sixteenth, twenty-first, thirtieth, fortieth, or fiftieth, read appropriate paragraphs in the numerology section below. If your ceremony is not for one of the special birthdays, please skip down to the paragraph following the special birthday section.

NUMEROLOGY

Numerology speaks to the symbolism around numbers. Numerology is typically used to determine the personality or characteristics of a person based on her year of birth. Adding up all of the digits in the day, month, and year of that person's birthday arrives at that number. The digits that make up the number resulting from that equation are further added together until it is reduced down to one digit. For example, for a person born on January 1, 1965, you would add together $1 + 1 + 1 + 9 + 6 + 5$, which equals 23. When you add $2 + 3$, you get the number 5. Everything in the world resonates at a specific frequency, and numbers are no different. The basic symbolism of numbers 1 through 9 is generally accepted in the field of numerology. In this particular instance, we use these simple, basic symbols to arrive at the vibration, which surrounds the personality, of the birthday in question. In this case the number _____ *[fill in birthday girl's age]*. This number represents the influences that _____ *[birthday girl]* will be working with this year. It is also a foreshadowing of possible opportunities waiting to make themselves available to her.

Choose appropriate birthday and read one of the following paragraphs out loud.

SIXTEENTH BIRTHDAY

When 1 and 6 are added together, you get the number 7. The energy around the number 7 is one of introspection and analysis, of a spiritual search for truth. Wisdom is a key word here. The other side of the number 7 is a tendency toward criticism of you or others as well as an inclination to suppress certain feelings. Now that you know what to expect, you are in a position to make choices that will move you in a positive forward motion or not. Predispositions, inclinations, and tendencies are just that. Leaning in one direction or another is up to you. Forewarned is forearmed!

TWENTY-FIRST BIRTHDAY

When 2 and 1 are added together, you get the number 3. The energy around the number 3 is one of joy and appreciation for life, of creativity, self-expression, and optimism. The other side of the number 3 is a tendency toward shallowness and excessiveness. Now that you know what to expect, you are in a position to make choices that will move you in a positive forward motion or not. Predispositions, inclinations, and tendencies are just that. Leaning in one direction or another is up to you. Forewarned is forearmed!

THIRTIETH BIRTHDAY

When 3 and 0 are added together, you get the number 3. The energy around the number 3 is one of joy and appreciation for life, of creativity, self-expression, and optimism. The other side of the number 3 is a tendency toward shallowness and excessiveness. Now that you know what to expect, you are in a position to make choices that will move you in a positive forward motion or not. Pre-dispositions, inclinations and tendencies are just that. Leaning in one direction or another is up to you. Forewarned is forearmed!

FORTIETH BIRTHDAY

When 4 and 0 are added together, you get the number 4. The energy around the number 4 is one of structure, practicality, and hard work. There is also a strong sense of service to others and loyalty. The other side of the number 4 is a tendency toward rigidity and authoritarianism. Now that you know what to expect, you are in a position to make choices that will move you in a positive forward motion or not. Predispositions, inclinations, and tendencies are just that. Leaning in one direction or another is up to you. Forewarned is forearmed!

FIFTIETH BIRTHDAY

When 5 and 0 are added together, you get the number 5. The energy around the number 5 is one of excitement, variety, and progressive thinking. Productive and positive use of free-dom is explored and adaptability comes with ease. The other side of the number 5 is a tendency toward inconsistency and excess in the realm of the senses. Now that you know what to expect, you are in a position to make choices that will move you in a positive forward motion or not. Predispositions, inclinations, and tendencies are just that. Leaning in one direction or another is up to you. Forewarned is forearmed!

End of special birthday variation section.

Although birthdays are typically celebrated with parties and presents, they are important for many reasons that tend to get lost in the festivities. The date of our birth is worth cele-brating because it gives us an opportunity to give thanks for the day we were given life, the most precious thing we own. Birthdays provide us with the chance to begin again each year; to get rid of habits, behaviors, and routines that no longer serve us; and to take on new projects that make us grow. That's why birthdays are a great time to perform cere-monies. The energy that thrusts us out into this world is especially strong and present on that day. It is there waiting to propel us once again into the positive flow of life, if we choose to tap into it. Birthdays are a great time to honor the self. To appreciate is to hold dear and what you hold dear, you treat with care and affection. Birthdays are an excellent time to reconnect with our five senses—the precious gifts of sight, smell, taste, touch and feel. And birthdays are a good time to remember the environment we were born into and to cherish this earth and to love it for its bountiful ways. And lest we forget, _____ *[birthday girl]* wouldn't have a birthday if not for her parents. So birthdays also give us a reason to honor and appreciate those who gave us birth, especially our mothers, whose lives were forever altered when they took on the care of another life with their own. So we will start today by invoking the mother goddesses of air, fire, water, earth, and spirit, and asking them to join us in wishing _____[birthday girl] and her mother _____ [mother's name] health, abundance, and happiness this year.

INVOCATION

We call upon:

Mother Goddess Lilith	Air goddess of the ancient Hebrew peoples, who makes children laugh in their sleep
Mother Goddess Parvatti	Fire goddess of India
Mother Goddess Isis	Water goddess of Egypt and Greece
Mother Goddess Odudua	Earth goddess of Africa
Spirit Goddess Demeter	Mother of us all

I will come around the room with two trays. One contains flowers, the other is empty, except for this white candle. Please select one flower from this tray and place it on this empty one. This means you are offering a silent prayer of thanks to your own mother and to our visiting goddesses for their life-giving energies.

Pass empty tray and tray-containing single flowers to birthday girl first, then around to each person. When everyone has had a turn, and the plate is full, read the following passage about candle burning.

If this is a solo ceremony, place one or as many flowers as you wish, one at a time, onto the empty platter.

CANDLES

Ever since primitive humans discovered that fire kept them warm and dry and made their food taste better, they went to great extremes to safeguard it from the elements. In fire they also saw a resemblance to the sun, whose rays provided them with warmth, and with light, which allowed them to face their enemies without fear. In this way sun and fire came to be worshiped as gods of protection from evil influences and spirits, and as gods of light, warmth, and healing. It is easy to see how these beliefs gave way to the practice of candle burning as an invitation for the light of God to come into a human heart, to purify and cleanse the environment, to protect and to take away the darkness.

A heartfelt belief in any one thing becomes reality for the believer. Centuries of belief in fire and the sun as beneficent gods have made them such. Passed on to modern humans from generation to generation, instinctively we light candles today for the same reasons. In the home, candles are burned to create warmth, to generate beautiful light, and to transform the environment, all of which have roots in the primal urges experienced by our ancestors. In ceremony, we burn candles in the hope of consciously recreating these now deeply rooted beliefs in the power of fire to bring us closer to the light, to help us attain enlightenment, and to prepare our environment for the gifts of the divine.

I am going to ask _____ *[birthday gir]* to light this candle. *[Turn to birthday girl.]* For just a moment, please hold our offering tray out in front of you, where we can all see it, before placing it on the altar. An altar is traditionally considered a special place where human beings can meet with God, your highest self, the divine, or that Great Mystery, or whatever term you use for the sacred. It is also a place to make offerings to deities whose favors and help you want to formally request. It is also an area designated to reflect the elements and intent of any given ceremony.

Take plate to birthday girl, hand her matches so that she may light candle. When this is done, hand the plate to her. While she holds plate out in front of her, read the following out loud.

Dear Goddesses: Please help us to acknowledge the sacrifice made by our mothers when they used their bodies as a vehicle to give us birth,

Open our hearts so that we might cherish the women who nourished us from birth, and whose care and affection continue to nourish us as we grow,

Please help us to express our thanks for the love, guidance, and best intentions of our mothers in our regard,

Please bless the offering that we make today to our mothers, to Mother Earth, to the spirit of motherhood that lies within each of us, and especially to _____ *[birthday girl's mother]* for bringing such a special soul into our midst! *[for bringing me into this world—variation for solo ceremony].*

Ring bell to signal the end of this ritual.

As I mentioned earlier, birthdays symbolize new beginnings. Much like spring cleaning, we get the opportunity to throw out the old to make room for the new. The next ritual will help _____ *[birthday girl]* let go of old or negative patterns, people, or situations that obstruct the positive flow of her life. In order to do this, I will pass around small strips of paper and pens *[or pencils]* to each of you. Please write down the thing or things you think might hinder _____ *[birthday girl]*'s growth and happiness. As her friends, we are in a good position to know these things! But if you can't think of anything specific, you can write down general things, such as "fear" or "impatience." *[Turn to birthday girl.]* Of course, you know better than anyone what you would like to surrender in order for this new year to be the best ever. If you need to make a long list, just ask me for more paper! When everyone is done, just fold your paper and _____ *[birthday girl]* will come around to collect them in this bowl.

After everyone has placed her paper in the bowl, empty contents into a fireplace, if there is one available, or into a heat-resistant container. Read the following out loud.

If this is a solo ceremony, you can either make a list on one sheet of paper or on several strips of paper, as indicated.

Dear Parvatti, fire goddess of India, we ask that you use your blazing flames to turn to ashes all the elements of _____ *[birthday girl]*'s life, that act as barriers to her progress. We are not asking that anything be burned down now—just trying to be clear—only that the energy that binds these things to _____ *[birthday girl]* dissipate back into the ethers from whence they came.

Hand matches to birthday girl and ask her to set pieces of paper on fire. When flames die down, wait until ashes are completely cold and pour them into a bag—plastic sandwich bag is fine—and hand them to birthday girl. Instruct her as follows:

You can dispose of these ashes any time and however you wish. Scatter them into the ocean (if appropriate), into the earth, into the trash, or into the toilet, and say "Bye-bye!"

Ring bell to signal the end of this ritual.

After helping _____ [birthday girl] to let go of the negative, now is the perfect time to follow up with our positive birthday wishes.

The power of the spoken word is great. Because we speak and use our voices every day, the power of our words can become diluted. However, when words are spoken with consciousness and intention, there is no limit to the string of actions and reactions they can unleash. This is where the old saying about being careful what you wish for comes from. All of our words, accumulated on top of each other, will become a tapestry of inspiration woven for _____ [birthday girl] as she faces this year's challenges. I would like to go around the room now and ask each of you to offer your personal wish to _____ [birthday girl]. Keep uppermost in your mind the simple truth that your will must be made manifest if it is inspired by love.

To keep the format easy, please say, for example "Dear _____ [birthday girl], I wish you love, or a new car, or success in such and such project, etc." Of course, if you would like to say more, feel free!

Be the first to present your wish, as an example to the others in the room. Then go around the room, calling each person by name so that she may state her wish. When everyone has had a turn, invite birthday girl to state a wish for herself as well.

For solo ceremony, prepare a list ahead of time of positive things you want to request of the universe, or just think about it on the spot, and then say them out loud. You can begin with, "Dear Universe, Please bless me with _____, and _____, etc." Make the list as long as you wish, but be as specific as possible.

Ring bell to signal the end of this ritual.

HONORING THE EARTH

To love, honor, respect, and nourish the earth that sustains us is to love, honor, respect, and nourish ourselves. With this next ritual, we will be joining our energies to help _____ *[birthday girl]* give back to Mother Earth the love and sustenance she receives from her each day. Some say that what we put out into the universe, we get back threefold, or that what we give, we get back. So, in essence, this is not a totally altruistic ritual because our actions ensure that the magical cycle of giving and receiving perpetuates itself, benefiting all who involve themselves in its momentum.

Here I have a plant, which symbolizes the earth, and two pitchers—one empty and the other filled with spring water, to which has been added several drops of different essential oils especially chosen for their specific properties.

HERBS, FLOWERS, PLANTS, AND TREES

The concentrated essences of the gifts that Mother Nature has bestowed upon us—her flowers, plants, trees, and herbs—are there to remind us of our connection to the earth. The life force that exists in human beings brings us the magic of breath. The life force within green, growing things also serves to nourish, revitalize, heal, and intoxicate us while bringing home our interdependent nature with Mother Earth. Endless numbers of books have been written on the medicinal and magical properties of herbs, flowers and trees. We use them here, fully thankful for their wonderful attributes and for their power to bring these gifts into our lives.

Lift pitcher of water blended with essential oils and read out loud:

The oils blended into this pitcher of water are:

Gardenia oil   For love

Eucalyptus oil   For healing

Lavender oil   For happiness and long life

Almond oil   For prosperity

 I would now like to ask each one of you to come to the altar and pour just a bit of this magical potion into this empty pitcher. As you do so, take the time to wish love, health, happiness, long life and prosperity to Mother Earth, to _____ *[birthday girl]* and to yourself by extension. Then I'll ask _____ *[birthday girl]* to do the same.

When this ritual is completed, speak directly to birthday girl:

_____, *[birthday girl]* please take the new pitcher and water this plant with its contents. Again, the plant represents the earth.

For solo ceremony, use this time to first prepare the first pitcher by placing two to three drops of each essential oil into the water. You will not need second pitcher. When you are ready, read prayer of thanks below and water plant. Leave it on your altar.

When birthday girl is ready to water the plant, ask her to repeat after you:

Dear Mother Earth, thank you for:
the soil on which I walk,
for the air I breathe,
for the fruits and vegetables that feed me,
for the trees that give me shade,
and the flowers that smell so sweet.
From the bottom of my heart, I offer you love.

Once she has poured the contents of the pitcher into the plant, ring bell to signal the end of this ritual.

Each year birthdays allow us to take advantage of that powerful energy which flows through all living things and which manifests through us as breath. Without breath, we have no life. It is that simple and that powerful. Focusing on the breath is the basis for many meditations because once we are able to join our breath to the in and out breath which sustains this world, human beings are lifted to an extraordinary place. This place has been defined as, among others, clarity, bliss, love, and union with God—or the highest self or that Great Mystery.

Form a circle around _____ *[birthday girl]. [Once circle is formed, read the following.]* Please close your eyes and take three slow, deep breaths. As you exhale, blow the air out through your mouth in an active way toward _____ *[birthday girl]*. While you do this, visualize your breath surrounding or infusing her with clarity, bliss, love, and all the powerful associations that come for you when you think about life force. For some of you it may be strength, for others it might be vitality. However you see it, give it to _____ *[birthday girl]* with all your heart. This energy can't help but propel her into this new birthday year with a bang! *[Turn to birthday girl.]* While we do this, I would like you to close your eyes and become receptive to these gifts, but by all means, join us in taking these three breaths. You can focus your breaths on yourself or on the rest of us. It doesn't matter, it all comes back around.

Close your eyes and take a deep breath. Everyone will follow your lead.

For solo ceremony, take as many deep breaths as you feel you need. Visualize the force that propelled you out into this world. Breathe it in as you inhale, and when you exhale, see it recycling back into your body through the top of your head. As you do this, ask the universe for clarity, peace, bliss, vitality, and joy!

Ring bell to signal the end of this ritual. Bring out birthday cake. Before lighting the candles, read the following out loud.

The custom of blowing out birthday candles comes from the belief that birthday candles, in particular, carry our wishes up to God. Please join me in singing "Happy Birthday" to _____ *[birthday girl]*. *[Turn to birthday girl.]* So, keep that in mind and blow these out with all your might!!

Lead everyone in "Happy Birthday." Note: If it isn't appropriate to eat cake at that time—maybe other food will be served first, etc.—it is perfectly okay to cut the cake later.

For solo ceremony, buy yourself a slice of cake or pie, or whatever you like. Place a candle on it. Sing "Happy Birthday" to yourself. Make a wish and blow out your candle!

END OF CEREMONY

FULL MOON

Filling Up on the Most Potent Female Energy

INTRODUCTION

E nchanting. Mysterious. Awe inspiring. Is there anything more magical than the sight of that luminous circle of light bathing us each month with her silver presence? We don't know exactly why, but when we look up at the moon we catch our breath, fill with wonder, and bow our heads. We get excited, feel a thrill, and gaze and gaze and gaze. We reflect and ponder, hoping deep down inside to decipher the moon's meaning, power, and influence in our lives.

Why do I say "her"? Mother Moon. Moon Goddess. Mother Goddess. Queen of Heaven. Eye of the Goddess.

From the beginning of time, in most ancient cultures, the moon has been described and revered as the feminine aspect of God. Astrologically, people who are ruled by the moon tend to be intuitive, passionate, deep thinking, dreamy, spontaneous, maternal, and sensitive—all typically female characteristics. Just as the moon controls the tides of the ocean, so does she direct the flow of a woman's bodily fluids in a ritual monthly cycle. In addition, she prepares the womb to accept the seed that grows, matures, and emerges as a new life form. This is the process through which the earth and human life are procreated, continue to recreate and evolve.

We—both male and female—sense the power of the moon's life-giving essence, and we want it. Associated with our feeling selves, the moon generates in us a desire to connect with our creative purpose and with the visionary and conscious being within that yearns to celebrate life, love, abundance, and fruitful productivity.

The waxing phase of the moon is believed to be a good time to ask for and to attract the things we need on all levels—spiritual, physical, emotional, and intellectual. The waning phase of the moon is the time to relieve ourselves of, to let go of, to give up, and surrender those things and aspects of our existence that no longer serve us.

The full moon represents us at our peak, at our most luminous. When the moon is full, it is the perfect time to connect with the energy that symbolizes us at our most powerful. On the day of the month when the moon is at her most glorious, most majestic phase, it is an excellent time to:

✥ Reaffirm your greatness

✥ Conquer your fears

✥ Ask for the moonlight to shine the path back to your strength

✥ Reconnect with your intuitive self

✥ Align yourself with your creative juices

✥ Ask for inspiration—you're at your most receptive

✥ Welcome abundance and fertility

✥ Invite consciousness in—you're as open as you'll ever be

✥ Fine-tune your psychic senses

✥ Get a read on your wildest, most spontaneous ideas

✥ Make friends with your sensuality

✥ Draw down, take in, absorb, and reflect that powerful lunar energy

✥ Celebrate!

An interesting side note: For years, the full moon has been associated with negative occurrences. In doing research for this ceremony, I happened onto the findings of three researchers* who examined over one hundred studies on well-publicized and generally accepted theories on the effects of the moon on human beings. They concluded that the studies failed to show any reliable or significant relationship between the full moon and any of the following: the homicide rate, traffic accidents, domestic violence, suicide, major disasters, kidnappings, violence in prisons, gunshot wounds or stabbings, crisis calls to police or fire stations, emergency room admissions, vampirism, alcoholism.

* Researchers Ivan Kelly, James Rotton, and Roger Culver/SkepDic.com

Not surprisingly, negative associations with the moon could not be validated. As usual, it is important to make the distinction between mythology and folklore, and media- or Hollywood-generated imagery.

The following suggestions are based on a ceremony involving multiple participants. Although a number of people may help you organize the event, one person should be chosen to lead the proceedings. If you want to create a ceremony just for yourself, simply adapt the instructions as needed.

PRE-CEREMONY PREPARATIONS

SELECTING A LOCATION
Ideally a Full Moon Ceremony is performed outdoors, under the celebrated light of the silvery moon! Front porch, backyard, a park, the beach, you name it. There's nothing quite so invigorating and powerful as allowing moon rays to wash over your body. However, for some, this may be impossible. Perhaps you live in an apartment building; maybe it is just too cold outside; or maybe you are ill, can't get out of bed, but feel an entreaty to the moon is just what you need. Simply pick a spot that feels good. If there is no moonlight to behold in your space, don't worry; you know the moon is there and she knows you are there.

PREPARING YOUR ALTAR/ITEMS NEEDED
Wear and encourage everyone to wear white or silver, if possible. Choose a table or a spot on the floor or ground on which to set your offerings to the moon. The following is a list of items you will need:
- Bell

- Two white and/or silver candles to decorate altar and one more white candle for yourself

- White chalk (represents moon) and black construction paper (represents night of ceremony)

- A white or silver cloth on which to lay out items

(CONTINUED)

🐌 Clear quartz crystal

🐌 Eggs (represents moon's maternal, fertile, life-giving, child-bearing aspect)

🐌 Flour or salt (represents moon dust) to be placed in small bowl on altar. Can also be used to mark the space or circle within which the ceremony will be performed. For this purpose, flour is best used in an outdoor setting.

🐌 White flowers (your choice) to decorate altar

🐌 Food/sweets (your choice) for later consumption

🐌 Gardenia incense stick (gardenia is white and attracts good spirits)

🐌 Sandalwood and myrrh incense cones

🐌 Matches (several books)

🐌 Milk (represents moon's rays in liquid form)

🐌 Round hand mirror (medium size)

🐌 Copies of runic table (see page 186)

🐌 Spring water in pitcher

🐌 Toothpicks (as many as there are participants)

🐌 White wine (represents the moon's rays in liquid form) and wine glasses

You may want to send an invitation to your guests. Include a copy of the introduction to the ceremony on page 63. Ask everyone to bring a white candle, a plate on which to place the candle, and offerings for the moon. Although appropriate items can be chosen from the following list (or the above list), everyone should be encouraged to bring whatever reminds her of the moon, her color, and her light, such as:

- White or silver candles
- Silver coins or jewelry
- Clear quartz crystal(s)
- Diamonds
- White flowers (like gardenias)
- Silver glitter/sequins
- Ice, snow, snowballs
  (if possible)

- Small round mirrors
- Moonstone
- White pearls or mother of pearl
- Pastis (an anise liqueur)

Place items can be placed on designated altar space. Individual items can be placed on favorite plates, platters, bowls, or in glasses. Also, prepare appropriate dance music (CD or tape and player)

BEFORE CEREMONY BEGINS

✦ Prepare altar (see Preparing Your Altar/Items Needed above)

✦ Place clear quartz crystal in pitcher, fill with spring water, and place outside, under the moon's rays.

✦ Make appropriate number of copies of runic table.

✦ Set a table with food, wine, and glasses for later consumption.

✦ Light gardenia incense.

✦ Light two white or silver candles on altar.

REMINDER: *Please remember to read through the ceremony in its entirety so that you can make appropriate changes. Practice reading it out loud in order to familiarize yourself and become comfortable with it. Most importantly, if the way I have written it does not feel suitable for you, or in keeping with the way you would normally express yourself, simply use it as a guideline for your own words where needed.*

PLEASE NOTE: All sections of the ceremony are meant to be read out loud, except for instructions set in italics.

FULL MOON
Filling Up on the Most Potent Female Energy

WELCOME

Welcome, everyone. Tonight we honor and celebrate the presence of the moon in our lives—her power, her gifts, her energy. The moon has long been considered the feminine aspect of God, and we come here hoping to connect with that part of ourselves which we see reflected in the sky—that highest, most intuitive and creative part. The moon energizes our ability to create, and that means create in every sense of the word—from creating life through our bodies to creating the life we want for ourselves.

Each of you comes tonight with a special and personal intention—the most important element in any ceremony. Through the acts we perform this evening, we will call upon the forces of the moon to make those intentions real, solid truths in our lives. That is the purpose of ceremony: to gather together our collective energies and to focus them on the fruition of our highest goals and dreams. We are here to help ourselves and to help each other. We are also here to give thanks for the fact that we appreciate and respect that highest presence symbolized right there in the night sky for all to see. We also give thanks for the special pull we feel to the moon and for her influence in our lives.

Choosing a predetermined time, place, and setting for an event; using symbolic words, aromas, sounds, and actions; and adding the participation of special people, all have the effect of lifting us out of our everyday frame of reference into the realm of the extraordinary, where anything and everything is possible simply because we wish it to be.

Though we might do some unusual things tonight, rest assured that they have all been carefully researched in the hope of creating our own version of centuries-old, multicultural practices that serve to make our communication with the moon effective.

I will start by purifying and clearing our space of any negative energies by smoking it with this special blend of incense. Incense is believed to carry our prayers to the gods. At the same time, it creates a pleasing environment for humans to commune with the divine. A specific blend of incense carries within it a particular dynamic, which when burned, is released into the atmosphere and converted into a powerful flow. When mixed with the energy of the participants, this force attracts specific energies, which help us to manifest our goals.

Incense is made up of flowers, woods, leaves, and barks, resins, spices, gums, oils, and herbs. Many aspects of our world are influenced by the planets, including herbs, flowers, plants, and trees. I have chosen lunar-influenced sandalwood and myrrh because sandalwood clears a place of negative energy and myrrh purifies the area by lifting its vibration and creating peace. I will first walk the perimeter of our circle with the incense, then hand it to you so that you can pass it around to each other and take the essence of these plants into your being. We don't only want to clear this space, we also want to clear ourselves!

Light the incense cones and walk around the room or area delineated as "your space," allowing the smoke to permeate the air. Then smoke yourself first. Do this by bringing the incense close to your face and using your hand to wave the smoke in. When you are done, hand it to the participant closest to you so that she may do the same and pass it on. When everyone has had a turn, ring bell to signal the end of this ritual.

Throughout the ages, the moon has had many names, including Moon Goddess, Mother Moon, Mother Goddess, Queen of Heaven, Eye of the Goddess, Goddess of the Moon, Lady of the Moon, Mother of the World, and others. In many ancient cultures, the moon motivated a spiritual movement that revered her important influence on nature. Tonight we call upon the Lady of the Moon in some of her most commonly adopted forms.

INVOCATION

Dear Luna	Roman goddess of the moon
Isis	Egyptian goddess of the moon
Inanna	Sumerian goddess of the moon
Asherah	Canaanite goddess of the moon
Akua-Ba	African goddess of the moon
Selene	Greek goddess of the moon
Hina	Hawaiian goddess of the moon
Chang-O	Chinese goddess of the moon
Diana	Moon goddess of Imperial Rome

We ask that you bless us with your presence this evening so that we might come to know you on more intimate terms, that we might each hear your special message, and that we might help in some small way to make your plans for Mother Earth a reality.

What we'll do now is a simple but powerful visualization. Please close your eyes and feel the light of the moon bathing your body. Imagine the moon's silver light entering through the top of your head, working its way down through your neck and chest, going down your arms into your hands, filtering down into your stomach and abdomen, further down into your groin, thighs, calves, and feet. Feel it pulsing bright and strong, filling your body with its rays, erasing all thoughts, concerns, and cares. You're making room for your intention.

Take time to do this until you sense that everyone in the room has completed the ritual, or until you sense that SHE has arrived. Ring bell to signal the end of this ritual.

Runes are the alphabet of the ancient Scandinavian peoples, and each symbol has a generally accepted magical meaning attached to it. Please take a copy of the runic table, study it for a moment, and then choose the runic symbol that most closely represents the wish, desire, or goal you want to see manifested as a result of this ceremony. Then take a toothpick and use it to inscribe or scratch that symbol into your candle. As you do this, remember to ask the goddess moon to make this wish a reality.

Make sure to have enough copies of the runic table (page 186 in this book) and toothpicks, so that they are easily accessible to all. When everyone is done, ring bell to signal the end of this ritual.

CANDLES

Candle burning is an invitation for the light of God to come into the human heart. In ceremony, we light candles for their ability to bring us closer to the light, to help us attain enlightenment, and to prepare our environment for the gifts of the divine. I'd like to ask each of you to place the candle that you brought in your plate or platter. There are several books of matches. Please light your candles.

After all candles have been lit, read the following out loud.

I ask you all now to make your offerings to the moon by placing them in the plate that holds your candle. Then please come up and place it on the altar. An altar is traditionally considered a special place where human beings can meet with God or that Great Mystery, depending on how you feel about that term. It is a place to make offerings to deities whose favors and help you want to formally request. It is also an area designated to reflect the elements and intent of any given ceremony.

Go through the items already laid out on the altar and explain the symbolic meaning of each, as explained in the pre-ceremony section, i.e., "This milk represents . . ."

Be the first to start. Place your offering to the moon on your own plate and set it on your designated altar space. Then stand just outside of the area. Ask the next person to do the same and then to come and stand next to you. You want all the candles and offerings to end up in one central location that you will all encircle. When everyone is standing around the altar and candles and offerings, ask everyone to repeat the following after you.

Dear Moon Goddess, we make these offerings to you because we love, honor, and appreciate your presence in our lives. We also seek your help in making our hopes and wishes come to fruition. Dear Moon Goddess, we thank you.

Ring bell to signal the end of this ritual. Pick up the hand mirror and read the following out loud.

This mirror, whose silvery reflection represents our visiting Moon Goddess, is a physical object meant to help us transcend the ultra-thin veil that often separates us from that most powerful aspect of ourselves. By looking into this mirror and speaking our deepest wish into it, we speak directly to the Moon Goddess here with us—the Moon Goddess whose light shines down on our homes this evening—and to the all-powerful Moon Goddess that we are.

Let's take a silent minute to think about what we would like to say to the Moon Goddess or to ask her.

Close your eyes for a few moments then read out loud.

As each of you looks deeply into the mirror, recognize the Moon Goddess in yourself and speak to her. After each of us speaks, we will take a moment to close our eyes and visualize that person's desire coming to fruition. You can do this any way you like, or you can simply imagine the beautiful rays of the moon surrounding that person and filling her up with success. If your question or wish to the moon is private, feel free to simply look into the mirror and ask your question silently.

Lift the mirror up to face level and be the first to start. After speaking into the mirror, close your eyes and visualize success. After thirty seconds or so, hand the mirror to the person next to you. When everyone has had her turn, ring bell to signal the end of this ritual.

Pass out a sheet of black paper and a piece of chalk to each person. Say the following out loud.

This white chalk represents the moon. The black paper represents this night. I would like everyone to write down her wish or goal—the same one recently spoken and scratched into your candle. When you're done, fold the paper and place it on your plate. At the end of the evening, everyone will take her offering plate home. If your candle has not burned down by then, you can light it every day, whenever you're home, until it does. Your black folded wish should be placed in a favorite box, your purse, your wallet, anywhere you like; keep it there until your wish comes to pass. It contains your energy, the magical energy of the moon, and the energy of this night. It also contains your intention.

When everyone is done, ring bell to signal end of this ritual.

Before we began tonight, I placed a pitcher of spring water under the light of the moon. In it I put a clear quartz crystal. Clear quartz crystals are very powerful for their ability to produce clarity or clear-sightedness, and to aid in the healing process on all levels. I am going to retrieve the pitcher now so that we can all drink from it and take in the essence of the Moon Goddess into our being.

Retrieve pitcher and tray of glasses. Pour from pitcher into each glass. Make a toast to the moon, clink glasses, and drink. Remind everyone to drink slowly and enjoy. When everyone is done, ring bell to signal the end of this ritual.

Bring out white wine and any food you may have prepared. Pour a glass as an offering to the Moon Goddess and place on altar next to candles and other offerings. Also prepare a plate of food or cake and place next to glass. Pour wine into everyone's glasses (same glasses as ones used for water may be used). Look up at the moon and say the following out loud.

This clear, smooth, elegant and festive wine represents your generous rays in liquid form on the earth plane. Dear Moon Goddess, we drink to you. We thank you for coming here tonight, for being with us, invigorating us, and helping us to know you better. We offer you this wine and food in the hope that you will stay on a bit longer to eat, drink, and dance with us as we continue to celebrate this magical evening and your wonderful presence in our lives. *[Clink glasses, drink.]*

[Pick up bowl containing salt and say the following] This salt represents moon dust. I invite and encourage you all to take pinches of it and sprinkle each other with it.

Turn on preselected and appropriately uplifting dance music. Invite everyone to dance! Eat! Drink! Celebrate!

END OF CEREMONY

RITES OF PASSAGE

BECOMING WOMAN
Celebrating First Menstruation

INTRODUCTION

Transition. Everyone goes through it. Sometimes it goes smoothly; sometimes it's like trying to dig yourself out from under a mountain of stones. Transformation, change, and growth—it all comes included in the package called life. A major shift in one's life occurs approximately every nine years. In the first nine years of my life, I left my home country and moved to the United States with my family. My teens defined the second era—a time in which angst and uncertainty about who I was and who I would become occupied much of my waking hours. The third lifetime entailed a move to a new city by myself, introduction to a deep spiritual foundation that would affect me on every level, and a first marriage. The fourth phase led me to another new city and a second marriage. The deadly boring work rut I'd been in for so long finally ended and I started my own financially challenging but successful and rewarding business. The last nine years have been filled with growth, expansion, exploration, and expression of my artistic self and lots of hard work in the introspection department.

Perhaps each of those lifetimes could have used a rite-of-passage ceremony. But none more so than those anxious, adolescent years highlighted by breaking out of puberty and navigating that minefield of emerging womanhood: developing breasts, femininity, and dealing with the opposite sex; discovering the power of sex and how to use it in a conscious way, plus, trying really hard to avoid pregnancy in the face of pressure and naiveté. Finding my way in a world filled with strong opinions and pre-conceived ideas about how I should be and react to things. Trying to figure out where I stood on issues and how flexible I should be. I could have used some help!

Indigenous cultures invest great time and energy in marking the passage from girlhood to womanhood. Some of the more negative practices involve putting the young girl in seclusion for a time because she is considered weak and vulnerable to evil spirits. Some cultures consider menstruation as a signal that the girl has become dangerously powerful to society, and potentially harmful to hunters and warriors. With all the jokes about PMS and mood swings and women "on the rag"—the connotation being "nasty" or "illogical"—it is easy to see how some of these beliefs seeped into modern society. However, most native peoples see menstruation as a wonderful and positive event. A young girl's first menstruation is seen as a "transformation" from child to adult and as a time to reflect on the new and exciting changes that come with this new status. The child-turned-woman is revered because she is blessed with fertility; she has the power to give birth and to maintain that life-cycle continuum. She is also believed to possess powers that are of great value to society, such as the power to heal and to bring rain. For this reason, parents will often bring their children to the initiate for her blessings.

In crafting this First Menstruation Ceremony, I wanted to focus on the sacred and powerful aspects of becoming a woman; to create rituals that might help a young girl accept, understand, and honor what she has become. In that regard, I feel it is important for the elders in her environment—her mother, older sisters, aunts, family friends; people she feels close to and respects—to share their stories with her and to counsel her. By counsel, I strongly recommend staying away from "shoulds," as teens (or anyone else) do not respond well to them. Much more helpful and respected are personal stories of discoveries, epiphanies, disappointments, and hurts. You might want to ask participants to think back to that time in their lives, of their frustrations and lessons learned, and to come prepared to share them.

Specifically, you might ask them to consider anecdotes that relate to the onset of menstruation as:

- A time to acknowledge woman's intuition—the special gift possessed by all women; paying attention to those strong hunches and honoring them.

- An event that signals one's ability to create life and to give birth on every level.

- A time to make friends with what it means to be a woman in all her aspects: as nurturer, healer, provider, decision maker, mother, friend, and goddess—the empowering "I can do anything" image.

🍃 A time to become acquainted with the process of bleeding; blood, what it means, its power and how to use it.

🍃 A time to prepare for the challenges of growing and maturing; choices to be made and expectations; relationships, their joys and disappointments.

Participants' stories should cover everything from friendships, first kisses, attitudes, communication issues, fears and problems experienced, how these incidents were dealt with, how they might have acted differently if given the chance. And they should remember to keep it light!

I remember being in an abusive relationship when I was eighteen. I was very much in love with a macho guy who was awfully controlling, and who often treated me with condescension. Seeing my distress, my well-meaning aunt suggested I read a book she'd found quite helpful called *The Total Woman* by Marabel Morgan. The crux of the book and author's advice was that in order to get a man to treat me well—in this case, with kindness and respect—I should accept his every decree and fulfill his every whim. In other words, do everything to make him happy, and certainly not to make any waves. In return, he would be so delighted that he would do everything in his power to please me and make me happy—basically, reward me for being good. I found the whole concept kind of offensive, but my aunt assured me it would work, as it had so beautifully for her with my uncle. So, I tried it. And it worked—for a time. Before long, he was back to being his old, nasty self. The bottom line was that my boyfriend was a jerk with a cruel streak and no amount of being nice was going to change that.

I recount this story because it is exactly the kind of anecdote I would have appreciated hearing before meeting my first love interest. It is the retelling of this kind of experience—while keeping it short and sweet—that can have powerful effects on a young woman, without going into the politics of game playing, subservience, and feminist theory.

I also encourage sharing tips and advice on how to deal with certain menstruation-related situations, from staining your clothes in public to answering questions such as "Why don't you want to go in the water today?" and from inserting-a-tampon-the-first-time tales to funny myths around a girl's period. A friend of mine soaks her saturated tampons in a glass of water, wrings the blood from them, and uses the water to fertilize her plants. This may sound nasty to some, but she has the most amazing garden I have ever seen! Stories like that. Stories that replace the beliefs of that "time of the month" as a "dirty" time, a painful time, and nothing but a curse. Some women say that they are at their most powerful when menstruating—stories that illustrate those kinds of things.

REMINDER: *Please remember to read through the ceremony in its entirety so that you can make appropriate changes. Practice reading it out loud in order to familiarize yourself and become comfortable with it. Most importantly, if the way I have written it does not feel suitable for you, or in keeping with the way you would normally express yourself, simply use it as a guideline for your own words where needed.*

PRE-CEREMONY PREPARATIONS

Invite women who the initiate feels close to, including friends her own age.

Ask everyone to bring an ornament as a gift which they feel will mark the initiate's status as a young woman, i.e., jewelry, hair decoration (feathers are great), hats, body or face paint, henna (for the artists in the audience), nail polish, make-up, etc. During the ceremony, each person will be asked to present the initiate with her gift by placing it or applying it on her.

Ask initiate to dress in white clothing to represent innocence and to identify her as special.

Prepare special dress or clothing for the initiate to change into at the end of ceremony. Initiate should be involved in making this decision. This can be clothing of princess dimensions or a favorite pair of blue jeans—whatever makes her feel comfortable.

Prepare foods that can be eaten cold or at room temperature for later consumption. Foods should include corn; some kind of meat, fowl, or fish; bread. Prepare dishes, cutlery, glassware, and napkins for later.

Keep the following on hand:
- White 8" pillar candle, One red candle

- Copies of runic table (as many as there are participants). Runic Table can be found on page 186 in this book.

- Toothpicks

  Items needed to make magic wand for initiate (feel free to add more):
- Tree branch or twig no longer than 18" in length—unless you prefer it longer

- Beads (Ask people to bring old beads they consider special, or buy new ones)

- Glue (try to have a couple different kinds of glue on hand, like cement glue and Elmer's, just to make sure you have the right type for the materials you choose to use),

- Rubber bands

- Cotton swabs

- Small clear quartz crystals (as many as you like)

- Herb mix made of powdered cinnamon, chicory, nutmeg, ginger, basil, and sandalwood

- A key (any key, old or unused)

- A few drops of lavender essential oil mixed with two tablespoons of vegetable oil (preferably not olive)

- Pink-, purple-, and teal-colored ribbons (length 18" or less per ribbon) can be satin/cloth type or the cheaper kind that you find at drug stores in gift wrapping departments

- Wishbone

(CONTINUED)

Select a spot or tabletop as altar. Place following on altar:

☙ White candles (one each for you, initiate, and guests)

☙ Flowers—roses (for rituals involving beginnings and their ability to strengthen psychic powers); or jasmine (self-love and self-confidence); or carnations (strength); or sunflowers (wisdom and manifest wishes); or any combination of these; or any mauve (intuition, self-trust, and self-confidence); or yellow (communication, creative endeavors, success, and joy) flowers.

☙ Small bowl filled with red wine

Any objects that symbolize woman, femininity, such as the following:

☙ Statuary or any representation of female deities

☙ Peaches, figs, kiwi, mango, tomatoes

☙ Eggs

☙ Photograph or image of pregnant woman or mother

☙ If available, photograph of initiate's mother when initiate was in the womb

☙ Perfume

☙ A hand mirror (to represent the moon)

☙ Rice

☙ Jewelry (pile a bunch of necklaces, rings, etc. in a pretty tray)

☙ Snake (real or artificial)

REMINDER: *Please remember to read through the ceremony in its entirety so that you can make appropriate changes. Practice reading it out loud in order to familiarize yourself and become comfortable with it. Most importantly, if the way I have written it does not feel suitable for you, or in keeping with the way you would normally express yourself, simply use it as a guideline for your own words where needed.*

PLEASE NOTE: All sections of the ceremony are meant to be read out loud, except for instructions set in italics.

BECOMING WOMAN
Celebrating First Menstruation

WELCOME
Welcome, everyone. Thank you all for coming. This ceremony has been conceived with love, and it is assumed that everyone here has come to bring wishes of love and support to _____ *[initiate]*.

CEREMONY
The stringing together of certain rituals performed with special intent is called ceremony. Ceremonies are important because they serve to gather up all of our energies and to focus them on one specific thing in this case, _____ *[initiate]*'s smooth and graceful transition from child to adult, from girl to woman.

　　　Choosing a predetermined time, place, and setting for an event; using symbolic words, aromas, sounds, and actions; and adding the participation of special people, all have the effect of lifting us out of our everyday world into the realm of the extraordinary, where anything and everything is possible simply because we wish it to be. Though some of the things we do today may seem unusual, know that they have all been carefully researched in the hope of recreating centuries-old practices from various corners of the world. These rituals serve to attract the positive power of the saints, spirits, angels, gods, and goddesses that surround us, and to make our wishes known to them. As you know, if you don't ask, you won't receive.

SAGE

I am going to start by smudging the room and each one of you with this sage stick*. To smudge is to purify with the smoke of sage branches bound together into a stick. Native traditions relate that smudging has the effect of removing negative energy and its remnants from people, places, and things. When I come around you, close your eyes and ask the universe to relax you, and to remove any stressful thoughts, fears, or worries.

Light sage stick with a match. Allow flame to burn for a moment then extinguish by blowing it out. It should start to smoke. If the smoke is thin, you may want to blow on it to ignite it further. First walk around the room, waving the smoke into corners and toward the ceiling. Then wave it around each person from left to right, then front and back. When everyone has been smudged, extinguish sage stick by placing it in any nearby plant, head first. Afterward, make sure to open a door or window for several minutes so that the smoke and any residue negative energy may have a point of exit.

CANDLES

There are a number of white candles here on the altar and I am going to ask each of you to come up and light one.

Ever since primitive humans discovered that fire kept them warm and dry and made their food taste better, they went to great extremes to safeguard it from the elements. In fire they also saw a resemblance to the sun, which provided them with warmth and light. This light also allowed them to face their enemies without fear. In this way did the sun and fire came to be worshiped as gods of protection from evil influences and spirits and from the rain, which destroys fire; and as gods of light, warmth, and healing. It is easy to see how these beliefs gave way to the practice of candle burning

* If sage stick is not available, substitute with sage incense stick.

as invitation for the light of God to come into a human heart, to purify and cleanse the environment, to protect, and to take away the darkness.

If you believe something strongly enough, it becomes real for you. Centuries of heartfelt belief in fire and the sun as kind-hearted gods have made it so. Passed on to modern humans from generation to generation, instinctively we light candles today for the same reasons. In the home, candles are burned to create a warm atmosphere, to generate beautiful light, and to transform the environment—all of which have roots in the primal urges experienced by our ancestors. In ceremony, we burn candles in the hope of consciously recreating these now deeply-rooted beliefs in the power of fire to bring us closer to the light, to help us attain enlightenment, and to prepare our environment for the gifts of the divine.

Candles can be placed in individual candleholders, together on a platter, or in candelabra. Be the first person to start by lighting a candle, then go around the room, asking everyone to take a turn coming up to light one. Initiate should be last. Hers can be set apart from the others, if you wish. After initiate has had her turn, read the following out loud.

An altar is traditionally considered a special place where human beings can meet with God, or the divine or that Great Mystery, or whatever term you use for the sacred. It is a place to make offerings to deities whose favors and help you want to formally request. It is also an area designated to reflect the element and intent of any given ceremony. So I'll just explain some of the objects we have here:

❧ There are _____ *[flowers chosen]* because…*[explain chosen properties based on information given in pre-ceremony preparation list]*.

- This bowl is filled with red wine, which represents the blood that nurtures us as we grow in our mothers' wombs, and which magically appears every month to remind us of our nature as women.

- These fruits were chosen for their symbolic representation of all things womanly and feminine.

- The eggs are symbolic of fertility and of the womb from which all life springs.

- Rice is another symbol of fertility and abundance in all areas of life.

- We have photos of a pregnant woman and/or of a pregnant _____ [initiate's pregnant mother] as representation of _____ [initiate]'s ability to create new life.

- We also have perfume and jewelry, accessories favored by human females and goddesses alike.

- A round hand-mirror, which represents the moon, worshiped in most ancient cultures as the feminine aspect of God.

- A snake, which in African civilizations, represents a woman's ability to regenerate herself through the birthing process, much as the snake is able to regenerate its skin. In some places, the snake stands for power, knowledge, and wisdom; and the medical community uses the snake as symbol for the healing arts, one of the many gifts with which women are blessed.

INVOCATION

By lighting the candles, we officially invite the light of God to wash over us today as we celebrate _____ *[initiate]*'s formal crossing over into womanhood. Now I'd like to invoke just a few of the female deities whose presence, energies, and blessings will make this event complete:

- First and foremost, I call upon Mother Earth. Of all the elements (air, fire, water, and earth), it is said that earth is the mother of all. Myths and legends around devotion for the earth as living mother are found in every ancient society known to humans. There has never been a "father earth"! Mother Earth, we ask you to bless us with your presence.

- I call upon Hecate, Greek goddess of transformation, who rules passages of life. Please honor us with your presence and extend your guiding hand to _____ *[initiate]* as she goes through this beautiful period of transformation.

- I call upon Lucina, Roman sun goddess who dispenses the sun's rays. Navajo Indians believe a new woman should pursue the sun's rays, which represent life, truth, beauty, and all else that is good. We ask that you come today and bathe _____ *[initiate]* with your generosity.

- I call upon Moira, Roman goddess of personal fate, who guides us in the direction of our lives. Please bless us with your presence today.

- I call upon European goddess Clotho, one of the three goddesses of fate and fortune, who spins and weaves the tapestry of our lives into a beautiful work of art. Please honor us with your loving talent today.

❧ And I call upon Erzulie, Haitian personification of beauty and feminine grace. We ask that you share your gifts with us today and with _____ (initiate) in particular.

    A First Menstruation ceremony is an event in which her community awards a girl the title of "woman." A level of maturity is recognized by the people around her, and it is an event considered meaningful by her peers. This is why we invite elders, people who have lived enough so that they can share the wisdom they have gained and you, _____ *[initiate]*'s friends, so that you can help celebrate this important time in her life.

    The first time a person menstruates is exciting. It means much more than the fact that the body is following its natural and biological course, and that you will begin bleeding each month. It does means you're healthy and walking down the road that every woman since Eve has walked before but what I mean is that this event is also important for reasons that are sometimes forgotten. And this is why we're here today, to point them out, acknowledge them, and celebrate them.

    A woman's First Menstruation means many, many things—some of them joyful, some of them intense, and some of them quite magical!

❧ The most obvious is the ability to bear children. (This doesn't come with the automatic ability to raise children, which means becoming aware of the responsibility that comes with this new gift.) But back to bearing children. More than having your own child someday, it also means that you now have the power to give life and to produce the life-nourishing fluid known as milk. It means that you are now part of the cycle of regeneration, which allows this world to recreate itself, to grow, progress, and evolve. It also means you can now re-create yourself. Didn't know you could do that, did you?

☞ To create. The ability to create means you are now a creator—a term which usually refers to God. I'll bet anything you never thought of yourself that way! As a creator, you can do more than create life for others. You can create the life you want for yourself. You are able to make your dreams a reality, to wish for something and see it come true, to decide how something will turn out and watch it happen, to change the course of events. Because women can do these things, at certain times throughout history, we have been called witches. I kind of like that word! What you do with your powers and how consciously you use them determines the type of witch that you are, or the type of woman you are. That power is in your hands simply because you are a woman. Use it wisely. Use it well. But mostly, just use it.

☞ Being able to create also means that you are a creative person. Boundless creativity is yours now. Creative is a term usually reserved for artists. You're an artist too! Your creative juices can be used to make art in the traditional sense of the word or to make art out of all that you do. Explore all your creative talents. What you do with them affects this world. When I say "world," I mean both the big world and the smaller world in which you live, love, work, and play.

☞ Have you ever heard the expression "woman's intuition?" Hello, you've got it. That wonderful power is also one of the gifts that come with crossing the path into womanhood. You know how certain people are considered psychic because they know things? The truth is that everyone is psychic, but only some develop those abilities; most ignore them. Women have more of those abilities than men do. That doesn't mean you should aspire to read people's fortunes. It means you can read your own. It means you know things—like the best choice to make in any given situation, the right road to follow when you're lost, how a friendship is likely to turn out, when a situation or person is dangerous, when someone is lying. You know those things; all you have to do is tune in to yourself, listen, pay attention, and don't doubt!

☞ Let's talk about blood for a minute—that other vital fluid. And bleeding. Contrary to everything you may have heard about that time of the month, when a woman is having her period, she is at her most powerful. As babies in the womb, we grow and nourish ourselves through our mothers' blood. Our blood is evidence of our connection to our ancestors, the first humans who walked the earth. It is physical proof of our own spirit. In other words, it is our telephone line to knowledge of ourselves. Connecting with our spiritual self usually requires down time, so it is a perfect time to rest and to reflect on the part we don't see when we look in the mirror. Although some of us feel weak or experience abdominal pains when we bleed, these are physical symptoms. Think of it as your physical body surrendering itself over to your spiritual self, which is strongest at that time. Bleeding is our monthly reminder of who we are. Exploring the mysteries of your blood is exploring the source of your power. Some women mix their menstrual blood with water and use it to feed their plants. Aboriginal women have been known to keep their blood in pouches and to use it for healing open cuts and sores. Bleeding is not a curse. It is a gift.

☞ Finally, maturing—becoming a woman and an adult means that certain things are expected of you: that you become productive, that you take charge of difficult situations, that you freely ask questions or advice from the right people, that you accept the consequences of your actions, that you treat people the way you would like to be treated yourself, that you behave in a kindly and respectful manner toward all living things, and that you stand by your beliefs but remain flexible. Being a woman means embracing your femininity and its loving, nurturing ways while questioning old concepts of what some think a woman should not be: a person who is independent, smart, determined, curious, a money maker, and a doer. On top of all that, you have to take your schoolwork seriously and find the time to party and have fun! You have your work cut out for you. We are here today to get you on your way.

I have asked the elders in this crowd to share with you simple, personal stories of their discoveries, challenges, and growth experiences starting from the time they got their first periods to yesterday. I'm hoping that in sharing these stories with you, the secrets and history of your community will serve you as you enter this new stage in your life. In other words, it's storytelling time!

Go around the room, until every woman has spoken, including you.

Pick up large, white, 8" candle; toothpicks; and runic table. Read the following out loud.

I have here a candle, with toothpicks and copies of a runic table. Runes are the alphabet of the ancient Scandinavian people, and each runic symbol has a generally accepted magical meaning attached to it. I would like each of you to take a toothpick and inscribe or scratch the runic symbol into the candle that most closely represents the wish, desire, or goal you want to see manifested for _____ [initiate] as she heads into this next life phase. As you do this, remember to ask our visiting goddesses to make this wish a reality. When you are done, pass the candle to the person next to you.

Make sure to have several copies of the runic table (page 186 in this book) and hand them out, along with tooth-picks, to each person. Hand the candle to the person closest to you. You should be the last person to inscribe the candle with a runic symbol, then hand it to initiate, who should also inscribe her wish for herself. Point her to a designated candlestick or plate where she should set candle down, then hand her matches, and instruct her as follows:

This candle represents the love and magical inten-tions of your friends and family for you. Please light it now. When the ceremony is over today, you can take it with you and light it every day until it burns down; or save it and light it whenever you feel you need the loving spirit, support, and encouragement of those gathered here today.

After she lights it, ring bell to signal end of this ritual. Please note that while each person inscribes the candle, it is per-fectly okay to talk and chat or do whatever you feel is appro-priate. This need not be a grave affair. The element of fun should never be too far away.

As I mentioned earlier, a woman possesses natural abilities to make magic—that potent combination of natu-ral, intuitive vision, focused intention, and follow-through. These powers we have, when used consciously, can affect not only our lives but also the lives of people around us, so they must be used carefully. Remember, never to use your powers for negative purposes or to cause harm to someone else. In fact, forget about affecting someone else's situation or behavior altogether. Always think about whatever it is you want to change for yourself. If, for example, there is a teacher you don't like—for whatever reason—any ritual that you do to change the situation should focus on what you want, i.e., you being happy in that classroom, you getting along with that teacher, you feeling good about your relationship to that teacher. Any use of your God-given abilities to change a situation by your concentration on such matters should never start out with "I want so and so to do whatever." Another person's actions are not yours to change. The universe gives you permission to change your life only in relationship to a person or situation. Put out what you want by calling upon deities or using the magical properties of plants, herbs, and flowers. Use your powers of visualization—because what you think about you attract. Do it any way you like, but never wish to alter the course of another person's life. Just put it out there and let the universe figure out how to do it. Now that we've gotten that out of the way, what I would like for us to do now is to make you a magic wand! Here I have a tree branch, which will be our starting point.

STEP ONE: What we'll do first is to pass the branch around to each one of you, along with this red candle. The red candle is symbolic of our menstrual blood, its power, and the mysteries it holds. I want everyone to take turns rubbing the candle on the branch so that by the time it's gone around the room, the branch should be covered with wax.

Start by rubbing the branch with the candle first, in order to demonstrate, then pass it along. Initiate should be last. When she is done, she should hand the branch back to you.

STEP TWO: What I have here is a mix of herbs that have been chosen for their magical properties.

HERBS, FLOWERS, PLANTS, AND TREES

The gifts that Mother Nature has bestowed upon us—her flowers, plants, trees, and herbs—are here to remind us of our connection to the earth. The life force that exists in human beings brings us the magic of breath. The life force within green, growing things also serves to nourish, revitalize, heal, and intoxicate us while showing us the nature of our relationship with Mother Earth. Endless numbers of books have been written on the medicinal and magical properties of herbs, flowers, and trees. We use herbs and spices here, fully thankful for their wonderful attributes and for their power to bring these gifts into our lives.

This herb mix contains herbs that can be found in many kitchen cabinets, but which are potent nonetheless:

Cinnamon	An amazing herb that can be used in matters dealing with healing, love, success, promoting spirituality, psychic power, and wealth
Chicory	To remove obstacles
Nutmeg	For luck
Ginger	For power
Basil	For protection
Sandalwood	To manifest wishes

We will take turns rolling the branch through these herbs or rubbing the herbs into the branch, whichever feels more comfortable for you This is in order to impregnate it with these powers. But first, I am going to have _____ *[initiate]* anoint or rub it with some lavender essential oil because lavender promotes happiness and peace. We also do this so that the herbs will have something to stick to!

Have initiate anoint branch, then hand it to back to you. Be the first to start, and then invite everyone to come up to the altar one by one and roll the branch through the herb mixture. Have initiate do it last. When this is done, pick up or point to ribbons and read the following out loud.

These ribbons have been chosen for their colors.

COLOR

Color is one of the properties of light. Dating back as far as 3000 B.C., astrologers, astronomers, and philosophers believed that colors give off vibrations, each of which is ruled by one of the seven planets. In turn, seven angels rule these planets. Science has proven that the human brain emits visible color vibrations known as the aura, which when studied, can give great insight into a person's character. The vibration given off by each color plays a large part in the physical world. It affects our decisions, our energy, and productivity levels as well as the way we feel and act. The use of colors in ceremony serves to summon the forces and attributes of the planets and angels associated with them.

I've chosen pink because it promotes self-love and can help you to become your own best friend; purple because it enhances psychic powers; and teal because it helps you handle whatever life throws your way. It also eases the decision-making process and aids in achieving balance.

What we will do next is glue these ribbons onto the branch. We can use these cotton swabs to apply the glue. I'll start by gluing one end of the first ribbon at one end of the branch, and then I am going to put a rubber band around it so that the glue takes hold. I will then pass it around so that each of you can take turns wrapping it around until it reaches the other tip of the branch. Remember to wrap it tightly and to hold on to the glued tip with your other hand while you do so. Feel free to go a couple of times around so that this doesn't take too long. Whoever gets to the end of the branch should put some glue at the tip of the ribbon to attach it to the branch. Then hand it to me so that I can put a rubber band around it to set the glue. Then we'll do the same with the other two ribbons. Please note that this will probably get a little messy. Expect to get glue on your hands. Also, it doesn't matter if the items aren't set straight in a row, or if the glue spreads around the items. We can always rub off the extra glue later.

It is fine to remove the rubber band from the first tip, glue the second ribbon tip down on top of the first ribbon, and place the rubber band back on to set the glue. Repeat as above until all three ribbons have been attached around the branch.

STEP THREE: I've asked everyone to bring beads that have a special significance to them, or clear quartz crystals. The quartz crystals are for promoting clarity. I also have here a wishbone, for making wishes come true; and a key for unlocking the doorways to the mysteries of the universe, and for openness of mind in general. Everyone should take a turn coming up to the altar to glue their bead and/or whatever they feel drawn to onto the branch. I would recommend that we glue as many of the items as possible on one side of the branch first because the glue will need a little time to set before we can glue other items to the sides.

Be the first to start and lead by example. Invite the next person to come up and do likewise until all objects are glued onto one side of the branch. Hold the decorated branch up for all to see, and facing initiate, say:

We are going to wait for the glue to set before placing the rest of our items onto the other sides of the branch. I propose we continue with this process while we begin the next phase of our ceremony. However, I want to say now that here today, the power of the love, good intentions, and energy of all of us present have transformed this simple branch into a magic wand for you. We offer it to you in the hope that you will use it wisely to transform your life into the special journey it can be simply because you are woman.

Ring bell to signal the end of this ritual.

It is now time for you to take the step that represents your physical transformation from girl to woman. Everyone has brought gifts that will help you make that conversion a reality. Why don't you go into the next room, change out of your whites and put on the clothes you've chosen to reflect your new status. One by one, we will come into the room and offer you our gifts by placing them on your body ourselves.

This is the time for people to place jewelry on her body, ornaments in her hair, paint with henna or body paints on her face or body, etc. While this is happening, you should bring out food and lay it out with plates, etc. for the celebration feast. You should be the last to go into the room, make your offering, then escort initiate out. When she is facing the crowd, lead everyone in applause. Read out loud.

Dear _____ *[initiate]*, we welcome you into our fold. As we have given to you today of our energy and love, we ask that you pass on to us some of your newly achieved power, grace, and wisdom by leading us into this celebration feast. You can do this simply by serving up the first spoonful of rice onto each of our plates. This is symbolic of your ability to nurture and nourish the world!

Have initiate serve up first spoonful of rice on each plate, then hand the plates to each person. Everyone can then serve herself and end the day's events by sharing food and drink.

END OF CEREMONY

GRADUATION

Soaring Without the Net

INTRODUCTION

ne of the dictionary definitions of graduation is the word *commencement*, meaning the beginning or start of something—a new life filled with the unknown and with opportunity. Graduation speaks to leaving the nest and fending for one's self out there. It's what young adults work toward for so long. It's fun; it's the END of school! No more exams and cramming for them; no more study dates, hours at the library; and fall never has to come again. Endless summers! Well, sort of. It's also the end of one particular road. Now it's time to explore one's own inner guidance, to walk away, not from family and the safety that represents, but toward a sea of choices, new people, and situations. It's risky and exciting, satisfying and stressful. Coping mechanisms certainly have their place in a young person's life at this time of exhilaration and spiraling emotions—a time that feels just like the sudden camera moves of an edgy, trippy music video. A ceremony dealing with all that is just what the doctor ordered.

PRE-CEREMONY PREPARATIONS

Select a table, mantel, or area as an altar. Arrange the following in an eye-pleasing arrangement:

- Amethyst stones in the rough (these can be purchased very inexpensively at New Age stores, crystal shops, or through the Internet)—as many of these are there are participants.

- One bell

Four bowls, each containing the following:
- Crushed bay leaves and alfalfa (enough for all participants to take a pinch)

- Dirt (fill bowl or container to the top)

- Stones (regular stones from a garden, beach, or park), as many stones as there are participants, plus five more for the graduate

(CONTINUED)

🌺 Fresh or dried or crushed red carnation petals (enough for all participants to take a pinch; or one per person, if single petals are being used)

I suggest that you make small explanatory cards and place them in front of each bowl to remind participants of the attributes associated with bay leaf, alfalfa, carnation petals, cinnamon oil and amethysts, as described in body of ceremony.

🌺 Small bottle of cinnamon oil (If cinammon oil can't be found, add a pinch of cinammon powder to vegetable oil)

🌺 Six white candles (positioned on a plate or platter by melting the wax at the bottom and standing them up so that they look like candles on a birthday cake).

🌺 Single-stem flowers (any kind, perhaps the graduate's favorite flower), as many as there are participants

🌺 Matches

🌺 Ribbon, string, or rope (to be used to tie all the flowers together)

🌺 One sage stick or sage incense stick

🌺 A scarf, cloth, or pre-made pouch or satchel

Ask all participants to come prepared to share a story or memory of emotions, situations, thoughts, fears, discoveries, choices, epiphanies, challenges, etc., which they experienced upon their graduation from high school or college. If there is someone in the group who never graduated, she can simply share a story of when she faced a new challenge or new era in her life. Ideally, these stories should illustrate the way these situations were dealt with, i.e., by accepting the available options, through a positive outlook, etc. The purpose is to share with the graduate that she is not alone in what she may be experiencing.

REMINDER: *Please remember to read through the ceremony in its entirety so that you can make appropriate changes. Practice reading it out loud in order to familiarize yourself and become comfortable with it. Most importantly, if the way I have written it does not feel suitable for you, or in keeping with the way you would normally express yourself, simply use it as a guideline for your own words where needed.*

PLEASE NOTE: All sections of the ceremony are meant to be read out loud, except for instructions set in italics.

GRADUATION
Soaring Without the Net

WELCOME

Welcome, everyone. Today we celebrate _____'s *[graduate's name]* graduation. She has worked very hard to get here, and she means to remember this special day forever. This is why she has asked you, the people she cares for most, to share it with her by taking part in this ceremony.

CEREMONY

The stringing together of certain rituals performed with special intent is called ceremony. Ceremonies are important because they serve to gather up all of our energies and to focus them on one specific thing, in this case, to help _____ *[graduate]* make the transition from student in the classroom to student of the world with confidence and enthusiasm, and with luck on her side. Choosing a predetermined time, place, and setting for an event; using symbolic words, aromas, sounds, and actions; and adding the participation of special people has the effect of lifting us out of our everyday frame of reference. We suddenly find ourselves transported into the realm of the extraordinary where anything and everything is possible simply because we wish it to be. Though some of the things we do today may seem unusual, know that they have all been carefully researched in the hope of recreating centuries-old practices from various corners of the world—rituals that serve to harness the positive power of the saints, spirits, angels, gods, and goddesses that surround us, and to make our desires known to them. As you know, if you don't ask, you won't receive.

Graduation is a time of change. It involves three distinct processes:

☞ Letting go of the structure that the educational environment provides to create fresh, new structures of thought and behavior.

☞ Accepting the new challenges laid out before you, like career paths, where to live (if appropriate), and new relationships. Financial responsibility, mapping out the roads toward self-sufficiency, and sketching out a blueprint of what life might look like in the future are of primary importance at this time. There is no turning back. There is no place for dread or fear. Accepting and embracing this new life phase with gusto is the goal.

☞ Once you let go of the old and accept the present, what remains before you, glowing and sparkling like a giant diamond, is the future. Moving toward that future with energy and positive forward motion is the last stage in this process of commencement, of new beginnings, of that graduation to the next level. And, lest we forget, there is still the matter of having fun, staying fit, partying, shopping, and resting. That's a lot to consider. This ceremony is meant to help get you on your way.

SAGE

This ceremony will begin as I smudge each one of you with this sage stick*. Smudging purifies and cleanses people, places, or things with smoke using sage branches tied together into a stick. According to Native American traditions, whenever the sacred plant of sage is burned, no negative influences may enter. As I come around you, close your eyes and ask the universe to make you clear and to remove any stressful thoughts, fears, or concerns.

* If sage stick is not available, substitute with sage incense stick.

Light sage stick with a match. Blow it out after a few seconds. Smoke should start to pour from it. Walk around the room and wave it around each person from left to right, then front and back. When everyone has been smudged, extinguish sage stick by placing it in any nearby plant, head first. Keep a window or two open so that the smoke and any residue negative energy may have a point of exit.

INVOCATION

In order to accomplish today's goals, I would like to invite certain deities to help us invigorate these proceedings. The Great Mystery often referred to as God takes many shapes, identities, and characteristics. We hope these deities from around the world will join us today and impart to _____ [graduate] the specific gifts and blessings for which they are known.

We call upon:

Lucina   Roman goddess of the sun and spring, symbol of rebirth. We invite you here today.

Hathor   Egyptian goddess of love, joy, passion, and merriment, please bless _____ [graduate] with your infectious zest for life.

Hecate   Greek goddess of the crossroads, who oversees all of life's passages. Please light the way to all the opportunities that await _____ [graduate].

Moira   Roman goddess of personal fate, who guides us in the direction of our lives. Please bless us and especially _____ [graduate] with your presence today.

Clotho   One of the three European goddesses of fate
                and fortune, who spins and weaves the tapes
                try of our lives into a beautiful work of art.
                Please honor us with your loving talent today.

Ganesh   Hindu god of wisdom, bringer of luck and
                prosperity, and remover of obstacles, we ask
                you to join us today. Also known as the pro-
                tector of knowledge, books, and education,
                Ganesh is usually called upon before any
                journey or major venture.

CANDLES

As you may have noticed *[indicate candles]*, this platter holds
six white candles. Each one represents one of the deities we
have invited here today. I'll just tell you a little bit about the
history of candle burning before we proceed.

Ever since primitive humans discovered that fire kept
them warm and dry and made their food taste better, they
went to great extremes to safeguard it from the elements. In
fire they also saw a resemblance to the sun, whose rays provided them with warmth, and with light, which allowed
them to face their enemies without fear. In this way the sun
and fire came to be worshiped as gods of protection from
evil influences and spirits, and as gods of light, warmth, and
healing. It is easy to see how these beliefs gave way to the
practice of candle burning as an invitation for the light of
God to come into a human heart, to purify and cleanse the
environment, to protect, and to take away the darkness.

A heartfelt belief in any one thing becomes reality for
the believer. Centuries of belief in fire and the sun as beneficent gods have made them such. Passed on to modern
humans from generation to generation, instinctively we light
candles today for the same reasons. In the home, candles are
burned to create warmth, to generate beautiful light, and to

transform the environment, all of which have roots in the primal urges experienced by our ancestors. In ceremony, we burn candles in the hope of consciously re-creating these now deeply-rooted beliefs in the power of fire to bring us closer to the light, to help us attain enlightenment, and to prepare our environment for the gifts of the divine.

[Turn to graduate] _____ *[graduate]*, I would like you to come up to the altar and light these candles. As you do this, keep in mind that this act represents your personal wish or prayer that deities join us here today and that they bestow their charms on you. Once the candles are lit, I invite everyone to close their eyes for a few seconds and join _____ *[graduate]* in a silent prayer of invitation to these benevolent spirits.

Once candles are lit and moment of silence has passed, ring bell to signal the end of this ritual.

As I mentioned earlier, the first step in finalizing the graduation process is letting go of the life you've always known.

In that regard, I think we can safely say that, literally or symbolically, these five things represent what you need to let go of in order to fully enter into the present:

School
It is the structure and environment you know so well.

Dependency
Becoming independent is what every adult strives to be. Independence comes with its own very different set of rules. It's time to let go of the old rules to make room for the new ones.

The nest	Whether you plan to move out soon or in the future, leaving the familiar home you've always known is inevitable. Planning for the creation and care of your own nest cannot happen until you give up the ties to your childhood environment.
The safety net	Deep down inside, you expect that the safety net will always be there for you should you really need it. However, there is not one gymnast who can ever hope to excel unless she fully embraces the reality that the safety net just might break some day.
Fears	Fears of any kind are always a hindrance, and at this time in particular.

Believe it or not, letting go of the things that no longer serve us does not only apply to new graduates. In life, we constantly accumulate things that hold us back after a time. In order to help boost _____'s *[graduate]* intent to let go of the person she used to be, I ask everyone in the room to think of something she needs to let go of right now in order to have a freer, more productive life. This could be a fear, a relationship, a bad habit or feeling. Here is a bowl filled with stones. I would like each one of you to take a turn coming up to the altar. Take a stone, let it represent the issue in your life you would most like to let go of, then offer it back to the earth by burying it into this bowl of dirt. Then I will ask _____ *[graduate]* to come up and do the same with five stones, each one representing her special set of issues. Our combined intentions will ensure success for us all, and especially for _____ *[graduate]*.

Be the first to start. Go up to the altar, pick up a stone, hold it in your hand for a moment as you visualize the thing you want to let go of. Bury it into the dirt. Motion to the next person, until everyone has had a turn. When graduate is done, walk to the altar, and pick up the bowl. Hold it up for a moment and say the following out loud.

Mother Earth, we ask that you accept all these things that no longer serve us and transform them into what we need most now in our lives.

Set bowl down on altar and ring bell to signal the end of this ritual.

Letting go of the old paves the way for acceptance of what life has to offer in the now. To accept is to receive willingly. For _____, *[graduate]* it means embracing this new life with all its challenges, responsibilities, and new relationships. This moment heralds an era of self-sufficiency, of enjoying the satisfaction that comes with making choices and taking risks. Accepting the present means accepting yourself as you are now, as you choose to be. To help you do this, I have asked everyone to come prepared to share a story about the time of their own graduation—about their joys, fears, discoveries, or difficulties, and how they dealt with them. It doesn't necessarily have to be at the time of graduation, though. It could also be about any time you understood that being present was all there was ever going to be. After each of you tells her story, I would like you to take one of these flowers and offer it to _____ *[graduate]* as you wish for her the most important thing you learned then.

When words are spoken with consciousness and intention, there is no limit to the string of actions and reactions they can unleash. All of our stories, accumulated on top of each other, will become a tapestry of inspiration woven for _____ *[graduate]* as she faces her own new world. *[Turn to graduate]* _____, *[graduate]* all you have to do to participate in this ritual is accept. Accept these stories and offerings for the gifts that they are.

Be the first to start. Share your story, offer graduate a flower, and say, for example, "Dear_____, [graduate] I wish you strength." Call on the next person to share her story until everyone has had a turn. Hand graduate a ribbon, string, or rope and read the following out loud to her.

These flowers represent our best wishes for you as you embrace your new life. Take this string and tie them all together. Let them dry and hold onto them. This way you will always have a physical reminder of our encouragement, love, and energy as well as the energy of this day. Feel free to pluck petals from it when needed and carry them with you when you feel you need a boost. Crush some of these petals and sprinkle them on a project (or even a friend) who needs an extra dose of luck; float them in your bathwater and soak. Get creative with them. They're yours. Use them as needed. Enjoy them!

Ring bell to signal the end of this ritual.

Enthusiasm, self-confidence, openness, vitality, strength, prosperity, and luck are the recipe ingredients required to make moving forward into your future the most delicious meal of your life. And this must be your lucky day because we are here to make sure your journey starts off on the right foot!

HERBS, FLOWERS, PLANTS, TREES, AND STONES

The gifts that Mother Nature has bestowed upon us—her flowers, plants, trees, herbs, and stones—are there to remind us of our connection to the earth. The life force that exists in human beings brings us the magic of breath. The life force within green, growing things and minerals serves to nourish, revitalize, heal, and intoxicate us while bringing home our interdependent nature with Mother Earth. Endless numbers of books have been written on the medicinal and magical

properties of herbs, flowers, trees, and stones, which we use here. We are fully thankful for their wonderful attributes and for their power to bring these gifts into our lives.
What I have prepared here is a mix of:

Bay leaf	For strength and protection
Alfalfa	For prosperity

In this bowl are:

Red carnation petals	For energy and vitality (dried, fresh, or crushed is up to you)

This bottle contains:

Cinnamon oil	For luck

And this bowl contains:

Amethyst stones	For self-confidence

What we are going to do now is create a special power pouch for _____ [graduate]. I would like to invite each one of you to take turns coming up to the altar. An altar is considered a special place where human beings can meet with God or the Great Mystery, or however you refer to that life force. Take a pinch of bay leaf and alfalfa and drop it into this cloth [or scarf, fabric, bag, etc.]. Then add a few [or, if crushed, a pinch of] carnation petals, and sprinkle them with some cinnamon oil. Finally, add an amethyst. As you do this, make sure to concentrate on asking the universe and our visiting deities to help make these wishes a reality for _____ [graduate]. When everyone has had a turn, I will ask _____ [graduate] to come up and do the same while making a silent prayer for herself, and then to use this long [string, ribbon, or rope] to tie it all together.

If there are many people in attendance and you think this may take a while, it is okay for everyone to talk. However, in order not to disperse the energy, it would be best if they limited their conversation to more personal stories or asking the graduate to share her vision of the immediate future. When everyone, including the graduate has had a turn filling the pouch, hand the graduate the string and instruct her to tie it in such a way that the pouch can be hung in a room or carried like a satchel.

Dear _____, *[graduate]* this pouch and all its magical contents is your physical reminder that energy, strength, prosperity, and self-confidence are always at hand, and that luck and good fortune are with you always. When you feel you need an extra boost of any of these blessings, carry this pouch with you. You can hang it somewhere in your room, keep it under your pillow or someplace special. It also carries our love and friendship.

_____ *[graduate]* and I would like to thank everyone for coming today and for lending your love, energy, and good intentions to this endeavor to kick start her new life with a bang.

_____, *[graduate]* we welcome you to your life as a full-fledged graduate.

Lead everyone in a round of applause. Play music, dance, eat, or whatever feels appropriate!

END OF CEREMONY

BLISSFUL MATRIMONY

Energizing Chances for a Successful Union

INTRODUCTION

T here is much activity, preparation, and excitement that goes into a wedding. But the emphasis is usually on the wedding, not the marriage. A wedding is a huge, festive celebration. Matrimony, on the other hand, is a daily adventure. It is an adventure that requires the right equipment and attitude, proper nourishment, fortitude and flexibility, team spirit, and excellent survival instincts. And, of course, it has to be fun! This ceremony aims to focus on keeping the path and destination clear, while the whirlwind of activity and excitement propel you and your loved one toward the beginning of the adventure.

Consider including this ceremony as part of the traditional wedding shower. Or you can perform this ceremony as a way to cap or bless the traditional wedding ceremony. You can do it a couple of months after the wedding—when you've had a sense of what areas could use a boost—or whenever it feels right. Remember, the intention of friends and family members that the marriage be blessed with success is the fuel and purpose of this ceremony. The timing couldn't matter less.

PRE-CEREMONY PREPARATIONS

🌹 Buy rosehips tea and prepare to serve in teacups at end of ceremony.

On altar (or chosen table, dais, mantel, etc.) place the following in an eye-pleasing arrangement:

🌹 Two white candles (These are to represent bride and groom in ceremony. Prepare two name cards for bride and groom and place each one next to or in front of a white candle.)

🌹 Two pink candles

🌹 One bell

🌹 One sage smudge stick or incense stick

(CONTINUED)

🐇 Bowl or container for dried flower mix of hibiscus flowers, orange peel and seeds, red rosebuds and petals, and henna powder (or leaves)

🐇 Bowl containing essential oil blend of ginger, cinnamon, and rosemary oils (Depending on number of guests expected, add ample quantity of any vegetable oil, preferably not olive, to blend, as needed. Just four to six drops of essential oil is quite strong. Adding vegetable oil does not dilute potency of oils.)

🐇 Two rose incense sticks

🐇 Fresh, red rose petals scattered on altar or placed in a container

🐇 One long-stemmed, fresh red rose in a bud vase

🐇 Pink cloth or handkerchief or scarf (does not need to be a solid color)

🐇 Ribbon or string

Feel free to add any other items you feel appropriate; things that remind you of love, i.e., hearts, photo(s) of the couple, fruits, crystals, a favorite jewelry item—perhaps even the necklace or earrings she will wear (or wore) on her wedding day; placing them on the altar will charge them. This is the time and place to make offerings to the gods!

Before asking everyone to gather in dedicated space, light as many white candles as you like throughout the room and burn one rose incense stick just before official start of ceremony. (It is OK if the pre-ceremony gathering and actual ceremony happen in the same room.)

REMINDER: *Please remember to read through the ceremony in its entirety so that you can make appropriate changes. Practice reading it out loud in order to familiarize yourself and become comfortable with it. Most importantly, if the way I have written it does not feel suitable for you or in keeping with the way you would normally express yourself, just use it as a guideline for your own words. This ceremony is written in heterosexual speak. If the couple in question is same-sex, use the term "partner" or "spouse" instead of "husband" or "wife." Additionally, the ceremony is written for a woman and her girlfriends. However, if it is to be a co-ed event, simply adapt the wording accordingly.*

PLEASE NOTE: All sections of the ceremony are meant to be read out loud, except for instructions set in italics.

BLISSFUL MATRIMONY
Energizing Chances for a Successful Union

WELCOME

Welcome, everyone. We come together today to celebrate the love, union, commitment, and special relationship formed through marriage. Soon _____ *[bride's name]* will take _____ *[groom's name]*'s hand to walk down that well-worn path. You are all here to help that path be the very best it can be, based on the love, support, and wishes of well-being you've brought with you today.

CEREMONY

The stringing together of certain rituals performed with special intent is called ceremony. Ceremonies are important because they serve to gather up all of our energies and to focus them on a specific thing we would like to see manifested: in this case, the fruition of _____ *[bride's name]* and _____ *[groom's name]*'s highest hopes for their life together now and into the future.

Choosing a predetermined time, place, and setting for an event; using symbolic words, aromas, sounds and actions; and adding the participation of special people, all have the effect of lifting us out of our everyday world into the realm of the extraordinary, where anything and everything is possible simply because we wish it to be. Though some of the things we do today may seem unusual, rest assured that they have all been carefully researched in the hope of recreating centuries-old practices from various corners of the world. These rituals serve to attract the positive power of the saints, spirits, angels, gods, and goddesses that surround us, and to make our wishes known to them. As you know, if you don't ask, you won't receive.

Coming up with the basic elements for a wonderful marriage is easy because some things never change. So, parts of the ceremony will focus on:

Love	Friendship	Respect
Trust	Kindness	Determination

But as times have changed, so have we—as women and as individuals, so I thought we might add these additional intentions and wishes *[address these next wishes to the bride directly]*:

- That you give each other the freedom and space to explore your individual selves. In this way may your relationship be made not of two halves but of two whole, well-rounded, and fulfilled human beings;

- That you help each other lose every negative idea you ever had about yourselves;

- That you work hard at communicating to each other your thoughts, feelings, and ideas—great and small;

- That you leave intransigence behind and learn to forgive.

While we're at it, we should throw in a good dose of humor, health, passion, and abundance in wealth, success in the workplace and in the loving support of your friends and family. How does that sound? If I've forgotten anything, there will be time for any or all of you to add your special wish for _____, our special friend, guest of honor and bride (to be), and for her chosen hero, _____.

BELL

I am going to start the ceremony by ringing this bell around the perimeter of the room. Three thousand years ago, in recognizing that everything in creation was imbued with a life force or energy, the ancient Chinese started practicing Feng Shui *[pronounced Feng Shway]* as a practical means of redirecting the flow of energy in a space. It created powerful adjustments that efficiently changed the course of their lives. Today Feng Shui is widely accepted as a natural way to attune oneself with the elements. This helps to harmonize, balance, and enhance the flow and level of energy in one's environment. The use of bells is prevalent in Feng Shui practices primarily to purify a space, disperse static energy, and to create a sacred circle of sound. This vibration and movement serves to ward off negative spirits and attract the angels. I use the bell here today for the same purpose. Please sit back and listen to its tone, allowing it to fill your being as your energy begins to vibrate at a new, heightened level.

Walk slowly around the perimeter of the room as you ring the bell. Repeat as many times as you wish until you feel a change or clearing of the vibration in the room. Once around the room is usually enough.

SAGE

I am now going smudge each one of you with this sage stick*. To smudge is to purify with the smoke of sage branches bound together into a stick. Native American traditions relate that wherever the sacred plant of sage is burned, no negative influences may enter. As I come around you, close your eyes and ask the universe to make you clear and to remove any stressful thoughts, fears, or concerns.

Light sage stick, preferably with a match, and then blow it out. Smoke should start to pour out of it. Wave it around

---

* If sage stick is not available, substitute with sage incense stick.

each person from left to right, then front and back. When everyone has been smudged, extinguish sage stick by placing it in any nearby plant, head first. Make sure to keep a window or two open so that the smoke and any residue negative energy may have a point of exit.

INVOCATION

We are here to honor _____ [bride] who is about to take [or has taken] the sacred vow of matrimony. She is about to become [or has become] part of a holy union in the eyes of her community, of all the gods and goddesses, of Mother Nature and most importantly, in the eyes of _____ [bride] and _____ [groom] themselves. No longer on her own, as she embraces _____ [groom] and takes him into her fold, her life will be changed forever.

To bless this union, we invoke:

Venus	Goddess of love and sexuality, who is traditionally celebrated every April 1st or April Fool's Day, symbolizing love's rule over logic
Lakshmi	Goddess of wealth and happiness
Lord Ganesha	Remover of obstacles, god of wisdom, and bringer of luck
Roman goddess Concordia	Personification of harmony
North African goddess Hygeia	Goddess of healing and illness prevention
Celtic goddess Epona	Who represents mobility to magical realms of existence

Egyptian goddess Who binds hearts together
Isis

    We also call upon the spirits and ancestors who inhabit _____ *[bride]*'s and _____ *[groom]*'s universe, who look after them, care for them, and guide them through their life's journey. *[Ring bell to signal the end of this ritual]*

CANDLES

Ever since primitive humans discovered that fire kept them warm and dry and made their food taste better, they went to great extremes to safeguard it from the elements. In fire they also saw a resemblance to the sun, whose rays provided them with warmth; and with light, which allowed them to face their enemies without fear. In this way the sun and fire came to be worshiped as gods of protection from evil influences and spirits, and as gods of light, warmth, and healing. It is easy to see how these beliefs gave way to the practice of candle burning as invitation for the light of God to come into a human heart, and as an invitation to purify and cleanse the environment, to protect, and to take away the darkness.

    A heartfelt belief in any one thing becomes reality for the believer. Centuries of belief in fire and the sun as beneficent gods have made it so. Passed on to modern humans from generation to generation, instinctively we light candles today for the same reasons. In the home, candles are burned to create warmth, to generate beautiful light, and to transform the environment—all of which have roots in the primal urges experienced by our ancestors. In ceremony, we burn candles in the hope of consciously recreating these now deeply rooted beliefs in the power of fire to bring us closer to the light, to help us attain enlightenment, and to prepare our environment for the gifts of the divine.

    You may have noticed these two white candles. Today they represent _____ *[bride]* and _____ *[groom]*. We are going to anoint, or rub, them with a special mix of oils that I have here on the altar. An altar is traditionally considered a special place where human beings can meet with God, or the divine or that Great Mystery, or whatever term you use for the sacred. It is a place to make offerings to deities whose favors and help you want to formally request. It is an area designated to reflect the element and intent of any given ceremony.

ESSENTIAL OILS

The concentrated essences of the gifts that Mother Nature has bestowed upon us—her flowers, herbs, fruits, and plants—are there to remind us of our connection to the earth. The life force that exists in human beings brings us the magic of breath. The life force within green, growing things also serves to nourish, revitalize, heal, and intoxicate us while showing us the nature of our relationship with Mother Earth. Endless numbers of books have been written on the medicinal and magical properties of herbs, flowers, and trees. We use essential oils here, fully thankful for their wonderful attributes and for their power to bring these gifts into our lives.

This essential oil blend consists of:

Ginger oil	For its power to bring love and to help boost the magical properties of all other oils
Cinnamon oil	For luck, communication, light-hearted laughter, and fun of romance (the lucky combination of ginger and cinnamon is that it has a way of opening others to your way of thinking!)
Rosemary oil	For acceptance, health, and passion

Pick up the candles one at a time. As you concentrate on making all of these wonderful wishes come true for _____ [bride] and _____ [groom]'s marriage, dip your hand in the oil and rub it all over each candle. Now is the perfect time to add your own personal wish for them as well. If you would like, you may do so out loud. When everyone is done, we will ask _____ *[bride]* to come up, anoint the candles and then light them. We will leave them lit until they burn down completely. If they have not burned down by the end of our day, we will give them to _____ *[bride]* to take home with her. You can light them every night until they burn down completely. Or save them and burn them whenever you feel the need. Our love and energy and good wishes will be stored in these candles, waiting to be released!

While we are doing that, feel free to share with each other any stories or thoughts you might have on love and commitment, what you expect from marriage, your hopes for the bride and groom, and your recipes for helping a relationship be the best it can be.

Be the first to start. Demonstrate anointing the candle with the oil, and then invite the next person to come up. When everyone has had a turn, and the bride has lit the candles, ring the bell three times to signal the end of this ritual.

CREATING LOVE SACHET

What I will ask you to do now is to help create a special love sachet for _____ *[bride]*.

On this altar are two pink candles. As I said earlier, the practice of candle burning stems from a belief in the power of fire to bring us closer to the light. Color is one of the properties of light, and the vibration given off by a color plays a large part in the way we feel and act. I chose the color pink because it represents love, romance, and friendship *[light candles]*. Incense is believed to carry our prayers to the gods and at the same time to create a pleasing environment for humans to commune with the divine. Each blend of incense carries within it a particular dynamic. When burned and mixed with the energy of the ceremony's participants, it helps us focus on why we have come together in ceremony.

The incense we burn here today is rose for its power to attract love and luck, for its ability to fan the flames of romance and friendship, and for its healing properties. The rose petals scattered on this altar, as well as this rose, are used for the powerful love-magic sealed within them.

In this bowl is a mix of:

Hibiscus flowers	For love in marriage
Dried orange peel and seeds	For prosperity and good fortune
Red rosebuds and petals	For love and passion, and for a vibration of joyful abundance in the home
Henna powder (or leaves)	For its legendary power to bring blessings of love, luck, and prosperity, and to ward off negative energies

I invite everyone to come to the altar, one at a time. Take a pinch of these dried flowers and place it on this pink cloth. As you do so, be sure to keep these good wishes for _____ [bride] and _____ [groom] uppermost in your minds. Once everyone has offered their energy and blessing into the flowers and placed them onto the cloth, we will ask _____ [bride] to do the same, and then to take the corners of the cloth and tie them together with this ribbon.

Be the first to start, and then call the next person up to the altar, going around the room until everyone has had a turn. Once the bride has tied the sachet with ribbon, read the following out loud, speaking directly to bride.

This will be yours to keep. Put it in a safe place and when you need it, take a deep whiff of it, squeeze it, or throw it into your bathwater and steep in it. Magically, all our love, support, good feelings, and intentions will be right there with you.

Ring bell to signal the end of the ceremony. Read the following out loud.

I want to thank everyone for your participation and attention, which has made this ceremony come to life. I've prepared a special tea made from roses, the flower of love, which I invite you all to share in while we get on with this party and _____ *[bride]* opens her gifts!

END OF CEREMONY

NEW BABY
A Welcoming Ceremony for New Beings

INTRODUCTION

New babies are celebrated in many ways—with baby showers, baptisms, baby namings, brisses, and other well-established ceremonies. Why do we need another, you might ask? Because this particular ceremony addresses many elements and issues usually overlooked in these traditional gatherings. Like the parents, for starters. Can a mother or father ever truly be prepared for the responsibility and total life re-evaluation that comes with a new baby? Probably not. But we can help launch their new and challenging adventure by summoning the forces that endow humans with tools like courage, patience, acceptance, and wisdom—not to mention money! If the ceremony is being held before the baby's birth, it is a good idea to focus, in part, on safety in the birthing process; the new mom typically needs emotional assistance from her sisters; the new baby can probably use the heavy artillery needed to embrace her new life and environment as she emerges, and certainly as she grows and matures. Strength of character, zest for life, capacity to love in the face of adversity, and to have faith in herself and the powers that guide her—we can help make those blessings real in her life simply through our focused intention to do so.

If you were planning to have a baby shower for an expectant mother, consider including a ceremony (this one or one of your own making) as part of the day's activities. Or, since there is so much attention on the mom and arriving infant at that time, perhaps you would like to wait a month or two or four or six after the birth to host a ceremony. Maybe Baby's first birthday is the perfect time to do it—when you might have a better feel for more specific tools she or he might benefit from. Or maybe you should do it simply when the time feels right. Trust in the power of your love-fueled motivation, and celebrate your or your loved ones' new family member with a special ceremony. Why not? You just can't beat a great beginning.

PRE-CEREMONY PREPARATIONS

- Send out invitations that should ask guests to bring a piece of fruit or favorite sweet as offering to New Baby.

Place the following in an eye-pleasing arrangement on altar (or chosen table, dais, mantel, etc.):

- Pretty cloth (if needed), preferably pastel in color

- One bell

- Pastel-colored flowers

Six small bowls for the following:

- Amethyst crystal (helps to keep you connected to self and others)

- Moonstone crystal (helps achieve one's heart's desire by seeing all possibilities).

- Several eggs (plain white or dyed red or combination of both) as symbol of new life

- Spring water, as symbol for purity

- Sugar, as symbol for sweetness and goodness

- Powdered incense mix for parents and powdered incense mix for baby (You may want to make placecards that tell participants which bowl is which and what herbs they contain, even though you will tell them the contents of each during the ceremony.)

- Seven candles, in the following colors: red, blue, green, golden yellow, pink, orange, white

- White candles (as many as you like to create warm ambience)

❧ Two charcoal blocks (the kind used for burning incense, not barbecuing), two small heat-resistant plates or saucers in which to burn charcoal and tweezers or tongs for handling the charcoal

❧ Two lavender incense sticks

❧ One sage smudge stick or incense stick

❧ Matches

❧ Platter for participants to place sweet offerings (size will vary depending on the number of guests expected)

❧ Symbolic baby toys (e.g., baby rattle), baby pictures of mother and father and/or friends in attendance

Before asking everyone to gather in dedicated ceremony space, light white candles throughout the room (as many as you like) and burn lavender incense just before official start of ceremony. (It is okay if pre-ceremony gathering happens in the same room in which the ceremony will be held.)

REMINDER: *Please remember to read through the ceremony in its entirety so that you can make appropriate changes. Practice reading it out loud in order to familiarize yourself and become comfortable with it. Most importantly, if the way I have written it does not feel suitable for you, or in keeping with the way you would normally express yourself, simply use it as a guideline for your own words where needed.*

PLEASE NOTE: All sections of the ceremony are meant to be read out loud, except for instructions set in italics.

NEW BABY
A Welcoming Ceremony for New Beings

WELCOME

Welcome, everyone. This ceremony has been conceived with love, and it is assumed that everyone here has come to bring wishes of love and well-being to _____ *[name of mother or mother and father]* and to _____ *[baby's name]*.

CEREMONY

The stringing together of certain rituals performed with special intent is called ceremony. Ceremonies are important because they serve to gather up all of our energies and to focus them on one specific thing, in this case, the welcoming *[and/or safe delivery]* of Baby _____ *[baby's name]*. We also come to celebrate _____ *[mother's name]* as she embarks on her new journey as a mother. Choosing a predetermined time, place, and setting for an event; using symbolic words, aromas, sounds, and actions; and adding the participation of special people, all have the effect of lifting us out of our everyday frame of reference into the realm of the extraordinary, where anything and everything is possible simply because we wish it to be. Though some of the things we do today may seem unusual, rest assured that they have all been carefully researched in the hope of recreating centuries-old practices from various corners of the world. These rituals serve to harness the positive power of the saints, spirits, angels, gods, and goddesses that surround us, and to make our desires known to them. As you know, if you don't ask, you won't receive.

BELL

I am going to start the ceremony by ringing this bell around the perimeter of the room. Three thousand years ago, in recognizing that everything in creation was imbued with a life force or energy, the ancient Chinese started practicing Feng Shui *[pronounced Feng Shway]* as a practical means of redirecting the flow of energy in a space. It created powerful adjustments that efficiently changed the course of their life. Today Feng Shui is widely accepted as a natural way to attune oneself with the elements. This helps to harmonize, balance, and enhance the flow and level of energy in one's environment. The use of bells is prevalent in Feng Shui practices primarily to purify a space, disperse static energy, and to create a sacred circle of sound. This vibration and movement serves to ward off negative spirits and to attract the angels. We use the bell here today for the same purpose. Please listen to its tone. Let it fill your being as you allow your energy to vibrate at a new, heightened level.

Walk slowly around perimeter of the room as you ring the bell. Repeat as many times as you wish until you feel a change or clearing of the vibration in the room. Once around the room is usually enough.

SAGE

I am now going to purify everyone's aura by smudging each one of you with this sage stick*. To smudge is to purify with smoke using sage branches tied together into a stick. Native American traditions relate that wherever the sacred plant of sage is burned, no negative influences may enter. As I come around you, close your eyes and ask the universe to make you clear and to remove any stressful thoughts, fears, or concerns.

Light sage stick with a match. Blow it out after a few seconds. Smoke should start to pour from it. Walk around the room and wave it around each person from left to right, then front and

* If sage stick is not available, substitute with sage incense stick.

back. When everyone has been smudged, extinguish sage stick by placing it in any nearby plant, head first. Make sure to keep a window or two open so that the smoke and any residue negative energy may have a point of exit.

INVOCATION

We are here to honor _____ *[mother's name]* who will be a mother. As she becomes the mother queen, the life she has known will forever be altered. No longer a girl, and with the wisdom that comes through growth, she takes on the care of another life with her own. Today we invoke the mother goddesses of air, fire, water, earth, and spirit and ask them to join us in wishing _____ *[mother's name]* a safe birth, *[or if child has already been born, whatever is appropriate]* a strong child, and happiness in motherhood.

We call upon:

Mother Goddess Lilith	Air goddess of the ancient Hebrew peoples, who makes children laugh in their sleep
Mother Goddess Parvatti	Fire goddess of India
Mother Goddess Isis	Water goddess of Egypt and Greece
Mother Goddess Odudua	Earth goddess of Africa
Spirit Goddess Demeter	Mother of us all

We also call upon the spirits who inhabit _____ *[mother's name]*'s and _____ *[father's name]*'s universe, who look after them, care for them, and guide them through their life's journey.

CANDLES

You may have noticed these unlit candles. They are an important part of today's proceedings, and they are here for a very specific reason.

Ever since primitive humans discovered that fire kept them warm and dry and made their food taste better, they went to great extremes to safeguard it from the elements. In fire they also saw a resemblance to the sun, whose rays provided them with warmth, and with light, which allowed them to face their enemies without fear. In this way the sun and fire came to be worshiped as gods of protection from evil influences and spirits and as gods of light, warmth, and healing. It is easy to see how these beliefs gave way to the practice of candle burning as an invitation for the light of God to come into a human heart, to purify and cleanse the environment, to protect, and to take away the darkness.

A heartfelt belief in any one thing becomes reality for the believer. Centuries of belief in fire and the sun as beneficent gods have made them such. Passed on to modern humans from generation to generation, instinctively we light candles today for the same reasons. In the home, candles are burned to create warmth, to generate beautiful light, and to transform the environment—all of which have roots in the primal urges experienced by our ancestors. In ceremony, we burn candles in the hope of consciously re-creating these now deeply rooted beliefs in the power of fire to bring us closer to the light, to help us attain enlightenment, and to prepare our environment for the gifts of the divine.

COLOR

Color is one of the properties of light. Dating back as far as 3000 B.C., astrologers, astronomers, and philosophers believed that colors give off vibrations, each of which is ruled by one of the seven planets. In turn seven planetary angels rule these planets. Science has proven that the human brain emits visible color vibrations known as the aura, which when studied, can give great insight into a person's character.

The vibration given off by each color plays a large part in the physical world. It affects the way we feel and act, our decisions, our energy and productivity levels. The use of colors in ceremony, often through the burning of specifically colored candles, serves to summon the forces and attributes of the planets and angels associated with them.

I will light these candles now, which have been chosen for their colors. As I do so, I will tell you the significance of each color, then ask you to close your eyes for a moment and join me in wishing these benefits to Baby _____. You can do this by visualizing Baby _____ or _____'s *[mother's name]* beautiful, ripe stomach surrounded by or infused with that color while asking our visiting goddesses to bless him/her with these gifts:

Red	For life, vitality, and luck
Blue	For healing powers, spiritual development and protection
Green	For fertility, prosperity, and gain of money
Golden Yellow	For intellectual development and strength of mind
Pink	For love, friendship, and happiness
Orange	For optimism and success
White	For psychic development, dispelling of evil influences, and protection

Color order of candles can vary, as you wish. After lighting each candle, stop, close your eyes, and visualize yourself what you have asked the participants to do before moving on to the next one. It is not necessary to dwell for a long period of time on these visualizations. It is important to keep the energy level up and the ceremony moving.

Ring bell to signal the end of the candle-lighting part of the ceremony.

PERSONAL WISHES

The power of the spoken word is great. Because we speak and use our voices every day, the power of our words can become diluted. However, when words are spoken with conscious-ness and intention, there is no limit to the string of actions and reactions they can unleash. This is where the old saying about being careful what you wish for comes from. I would like to go around the room now and ask each of you to offer your personal wish to Baby _____ *[baby's name]*. Keep uppermost in your mind the simple truth that your will must be made manifest if it is inspired by love. All of our words, accumulated on top of each other, will become a tapestry of inspiration woven for Baby _____ *[baby's name]* as she faces life's challenges. To keep the format easy, please say, for example "Dear Baby _____ *[baby's name]*, I wish you kindness." Of course, if you would like to say more, feel free!

Be the first to present your wish as an example to the oth-ers in the room. Then go around the room, calling each per-son by name so that she may state her wish.

HERBS, FLOWERS, PLANTS, AND TREES

The gifts that Mother Nature has bestowed upon us—her flowers, plants, trees, and herbs—are there to remind us of our connection to the earth. The life force that exists in human beings brings us the magic of breath. The life force within green, growing things also serves to nourish, revital-ize, heal, and intoxicate us while bringing home our inter-dependent nature with Mother Earth. Endless numbers of books have been written on the medicinal and magical properties of herbs, flowers, and trees which we use. We are fully thankful for their wonderful attributes and for their power to bring these gifts into our lives.

Flowers, woods, leaves, barks, resins, spices, gums, oils, and herbs have for centuries been blended together to create incense. Incense is believed to carry our prayers to the gods and at the same time to create a pleasing environment for humans to commune with the divine. When burned, it also encourages us to enter the state of consciousness necessary to awaken our own energies and to direct them toward the reason we have come together in ceremony. Each blend of incense, with its special mix of extracts carries within it a particular dynamic. When burned, it is released into the atmosphere and converted into a powerful flow. This force, when mixed with the energy of the ceremony's participants, attracts specific energies, which help us manifest our goal.

What we have here today is a special combination of herbs, ground down into powder for incense purposes. There are two bowls, each filled with special incense mixes specifically designed to deal with the day-to-day issues of life, because we don't want to forget those. One bowl holds incense for _____ [name(s) of mother or mother and father]. It is made up of:

Basil	For prosperity (because they'll need it)
Lavender	For love and an easy childbirth
Bay leaf	For strength
Hazel	For wisdom
Chamomile	For patience (because they'll definitely need that!)

The second bowl is for Baby _____ *[baby's name]* and it contains:

Rosemary   For beauty

Thyme   For courage

Passionflower   For anger management

Mint   For health

Cinnamon   So that he/she will be a considerate and exciting lover

I will ask you now to come to the altar, which is traditionally considered a special place where human beings can meet with God, the divine, that Great Mystery, or whatever term you use for the sacred. It is also a place to make offerings to deities whose favors and help you want to formally request. It is an area designated to reflect the elements and intent of any given ceremony. *[You may want to explain the items on the altar and their symbolic meanings.]*

I invite you to come to the altar at your own pace and to throw a pinch of powdered incense from each bowl onto the burning charcoal block placed in front of it. As you do this, remember to ask our visiting goddesses for their help in bringing these wishes for the family to fruition.

There is also a large platter on the altar. Please place your sweet offerings on it. They are a symbol of your personal wish for Baby _____ *[baby's name]* to have a sweeter life.

FORMAL ENDING

[You may use either the formal or informal ending, whichever you prefer.] _____ *[mother's name]* and I thank you all so much for coming here today. We thank the goddesses, spirits,

and friends of nature who have come to help us celebrate this birth. We ask that they stay close to us all on our life's journey, and especially on Baby _____'s *[baby's name]* path of growth, transformation, and elevation to the new journey that awaits him/her beyond.

> *You should be the first to start. Light charcoal block by picking it up with tweezers or tongs and holding a match to the edge. When you see it start to spark, that means it is ready or hot enough. Place the block down on your small heat-resistant plate, then, using your fingers, take a pinch of powdered incense from the first bowl and place it onto a charcoal block. It will smoke a little. Move to the second bowl of incense and charcoal block and do the same. Invite the next person to come up. Everyone can step up to the altar as the mother begins to open her presents—if presents are in order.*

INFORMAL ENDING

I have found that often, at the end of a ceremony, people will naturally disperse without the need for a formal ending. This is quite all right. In fact, you may sense people's attention spans waning before you get to the end, in which case you might want to skip certain steps. This is a living, breathing process, which works with the energy in the room. This particular ceremony may be too long if it is a very large gathering. If this is the case, you might want to do a general smudging around the room with the sage stick rather than around each person. You should feel free to tailor-make the ceremony to your specific need or situation. If your ceremony ends informally, simply thank everyone for coming.

END OF CEREMONY

THE HEART MOVES ON

Healing the Wounds of Divorce

INTRODUCTION

I have unfortunately been through a divorce. Like murder, abortion, and rape, divorce is one of those ugly words in our vocabulary. No matter what, it's one of those experiences everyone would prefer to avoid. But unfortunately divorce happens, and more and more, it seems. Dealing with the plethora of agonizing emotions that come with it is more than enough reason to create rituals that help to make it easier and smoother. When I first started thinking about this ceremony, I wrote down a list of words I associate with divorce. The words, which immediately started jumping up and down in my head like children clamoring for attention, went something like this: endings, separation, anger, closure, disappointment, letting go. I let those words tumble around in my brain for a day or so, thinking about them and what I could offer as suggestions for dealing with them. But then another idea started trying to crash this particularly sad party—an idea that revolved around more expansive issues, like new beginnings, transition, openings, opportunity, change, growth. I liked that idea. I made room for it, welcomed it, and allowed it to throw its weight around a little. After another few days of letting those two thoughts rummage around in my mind, a third idea presented itself. This one centered on relationships, their successes and failures, and what we can learn from them. First of all, should we measure a marriage simply on the basis of longevity? As human beings, we are used to the idea of endings: "things end," "everything ends," "everything changes." These common expressions lend themselves to multiple life situations. We know that strong ideas or opinions end, and others come in to replace them; that jobs end and new opportunities develop; that addresses, friendships, tastes in style, food, and music usually change at some point, and that other fresh choices take over. We don't necessarily see those situations as negative. Why, then, do we see the end of a marriage as a failure on our part? Why should we measure the success of a marriage on whether it lasts forever? There is much to be said for long-term relationships: the opportunity they give us to learn about ourselves through the ever-present mirror of another human being; the chance we are given to learn the ways of love, and the complexities of the human heart; the options we are offered, like a smorgasbord, around the issues of compromise, sharing, the art of listening, communication, forgiveness, and so much more. So the success or collapse of a marriage should not revolve around how it lasts, but how much we learn from it, how much we grow and evolve as a result of it. Like close friends, cherished family members, or important teachers, you and your soulmate may one day part from each other. It will be sad; there may be feelings of betrayal, hurt, jealousy, or anger. But the actual act of parting need not, and, yes, I'll say it, should not be a reflection on you as a person, or on your ability to succeed within the context of a relationship. After all, your new soulmate—the one for this other person you've become, the one with new tastes, opinions, career or lifestyle—is just waiting for his or her moment to arrive.

PRE-CEREMONY PREPARATIONS

Depending on the relationship between you and your former spouse, you may want to do a ceremony together. However, this ceremony is intended for you and friends who support you and want to help you through this transition. Invite accordingly. I have written the ceremony for a woman, and all pronouns reflect this. It is impossible to write a generic ceremony for divorce, so I have chosen to focus on the feelings that eventually surface, regardless of any given situation. For example, no matter why people choose to separate, there are inevitable feelings of sadness. The reasons and issues surrounding each breakup are very personal. In some cases, there may have been abuse or threats of physical danger; in others there may have been infidelity or other acts of betrayal. Some divorces are a relief to both parties; and in certain instances, there is still much love between the people involved. For this reason, it is crucial that you read through the entire ceremony beforehand and tailor the words I have written to suit your particular circumstance. Insert or delete comments as needed. The ceremony is written in the first person because, oftentimes, it is the person going through the process who knows just how much help she needs. However, if the person reading this book would like to host a ceremony for a close friend who is going through or has or recently gone through a divorce, all you need to do is change the first-person pronouns to the third person or the person's name. And finally, the ceremony is written in hetero-sexual speak. If the couple in question is same-sex, simply use the term "partner "or "spouse" instead of "husband" or" wife."

Please consider the following suggestions in preparation for your ceremony:

✎ Divorcée should start out by wearing black (the color of endings and separation) and later change into something red (the color of taking charge of difficult situations and strength, vitality, and energy).

Prepare altar by choosing a table or area and lay out items relating to endings/closure, transition/change, new beginnings/expansion. Choose as many items as you can that deal directly and personally with the couple in question, the beginning of the relationship, its ending, and its new prospects. These items can include:

✎ Marriage certificate

✎ A photo of the couple (propped up or in frame)

✎ Wedding ring/engagement ring

✎ Any significant gifts given by spouse or other objects that represent something important within context of marriage

✎ Anything broken (ceramic, plate, glass, necklace) to represent breakup

✎ Small covered bottle, jar or container filled with vinegar (to represent feelings of acidity or bitterness present between couple or on your part)

All above items should be placed on one side of altar for later disposal into designated box, along with book of your married life, which will be created as part of ceremony.

✎ A large empty box (to store items representing past life with former spouse)

✎ Colored candles, one of each following color: red, light blue, gold, green, mauve, pink, silver, teal, yellow

(CONTINUED)

❖ White candles (as many as there are participants)

❖ Matches

❖ Book with blank pages

❖ 8 $\frac{1}{2}$" x 11" sheet of black paper (to make cover for "end of marriage" book)

Use white chalk (or pen that will show on black paper — perhaps silver or gold) to draw seal of angel Aratron and symbol of Saturn (these are very simple line drawings, found on page 187 of this book) onto black paper. You may draw them in any position or dimension that you wish.

❖ 8 $\frac{1}{2}$" x 11" sheets of white paper, punched with three-hole punch (as many sheets as there are participants, plus a few more)

❖ Two sheets of cardboard (8 $\frac{1}{2}$" x 11"), punched with three-hole punch

❖ Clear plastic wrapping

❖ String, thin rope, or ribbon (for tying new book together)

❖ Transparent tape

❖ Pens

❖ Two herb mixes: (1) chili powder, cinnamon, ginger; (2) frankincense, lemon peel, myrrh

❖ Vegetable oil in a bowl, in which will be added herb mix #1

❖ Small bowl, in which you will place herb mix #2

❖ Small bowl filled with honey

> ☙ Small- to medium-sized artist's paintbrush
>
> ☙ Small bowl filled with spring water to represent flow of life (transition)
>
> ☙ Pitcher filled with spring water
>
> ☙ Small plant and/or flowers to represent growth and blossoming of new life
>
> ☙ Another plant set off to the side (to represent former spouse)
>
> ☙ Appropriate number of wine or champagne glasses on a tray; bottles of wine or champagne or celebratory beverage of your choice

REMINDER: *Please remember to read through the ceremony in its entirety so that you can make appropriate changes. Practice reading it out loud in order to familiarize yourself and become comfortable with it. Most importantly, if the way I have written it does not feel suitable for you, or in keeping with the way you would normally express yourself, simply use it as a guideline for your own words where needed. Though this ceremony focuses on divorce, it can also be used for any kind of rupture, separation, or breakup. Just adapt the words accordingly.*

PLEASE NOTE: All sections of the ceremony are meant to be read out loud, except for instructions set in italics.

THE HEART MOVES ON
Healing the Wounds of Divorce, Dancing into the Future

WELCOME

Welcome, everyone, and thank you all for coming. You know what I am going *[or have gone]* through in regard to my divorce from _____ *[former spouse]*. I asked you to come because I feel it would be helpful for me to take part in a ceremony that centers on the challenging issues of divorce—both positive and negative—and I know you would like to help.

CEREMONY

The stringing together of certain rituals performed with special intent is called ceremony. Ceremonies are important because they serve to gather up all of our energies and to focus them on one specific thing—in this case, helping me make the difficult transition from life as a married woman into life as a single woman. Choosing a predetermined time, place, and setting for an event; using symbolic words, aromas, sounds, and actions; and adding the participation of special people has the effect of lifting us out of our everyday frame of reference into the realm of the extraordinary, where anything and everything is possible simply because we wish it to be. Though some of the things we do today may seem unusual, know that they have all been carefully researched in the hope of recreating centuries-old practices from various corners of the world. These rituals serve to harness the positive power of the saints, spirits, angels, gods, and goddesses that surround us, and to make our desires known to them. As you know, if you don't ask, you won't receive.

Divorce is a particularly difficult experience because it makes you deal with two sets of issues—the first being issues of endings, separation, and letting go; disappointment, sadness, fear, and trying to achieve closure. *(You may want to add your specifics, such as anger, betrayal, abuse, etc.)* The second set of issues involves acceptance and forgiveness, becoming open to new beginnings and new opportunities, welcoming joy and expansion. That's a lot. But with time, willingness, self-discipline, and the help of people who love me, I'm sure I can do it. This ceremony will give me the boost I need. It feels a little strange to invite all of you over to focus on my needs and me, but I decided to look at it, not as an act of self-interest but as my first attempt at taking the bull by the horns. And since bulls are known for bucking and resisting, I figure I need all the help I can get! I want to start by saying thank you for taking the time out of your busy schedules to be here today, and for caring. Your caring is the ingredient that will make this ceremony the powerful and successful jump-start I need as I embark on this new phase of my life.

BELL

I am going to start the ceremony by ringing this bell around the perimeter of the room. Three thousand years ago, in recognizing that everything in creation was imbued with a life force or energy, the ancient Chinese started practicing Feng Shui [*pronounced Feng Shway*] as a practical means of redirecting the flow of energy in a space. It created powerful adjustments that efficiently changed the course of their lives. Today Feng Shui is widely accepted as a natural way to attune oneself with the elements. This helps to harmonize, balance, and enhance the flow and level of energy in one's environment. The use of bells is prevalent in Feng Shui practices primarily to purify a space, disperse static energy, and to create a sacred circle of sound. This vibration and movement serves to ward off negative spirits and attract the angels. I use the bell here today for the same purpose. Please sit back and listen to its tone, allowing it to fill your being as your energy begins to vibrate at a new, heightened level.

Walk slowly around perimeter of the room as you ring the bell. Repeat as many times as you wish until you feel a change or clearing of the vibration in the room. Once is usually enough.

ALTAR

This table is our dedicated altar space today. An altar is traditionally considered a special place where you can meet with God, the divine, that Great Mystery, or whatever term you use for the sacred. It is a place to make offerings to deities whose favors and help you want to formally request. It is also an area designated to reflect the elements and intent of any given ceremony.

CANDLES

[Point to white candle] Ever since primitive humans discovered that fire kept them warm and dry and made their food taste better, they went to great extremes to safeguard it from the elements. In fire they also saw a resemblance to the sun, whose rays provided them with warmth, and with light, which allowed them to face their enemies without fear. In this way the sun and fire came to be worshiped as gods of protection from evil influences and spirits, and as gods of light, warmth, and healing. It is easy to see how these beliefs gave way to the practice of candle burning as invitation for the light of God to come into a human heart, to purify and cleanse the environment, to protect, and to take away the darkness.

A heartfelt belief in any one thing becomes reality for the believer. Centuries of belief in fire and the sun as beneficent gods have made them such. Passed on to modern humans from generation to generation, instinctively we light candles today for the same reasons. In the home, candles are burned to create warmth, to generate beautiful light, and to transform the environment—all of which have roots in the primal urges experienced by our ancestors. In ceremony, we burn candles in the hope of consciously recreating these now deeply rooted beliefs in the power of fire to bring us closer to the light, to help us attain enlightenment, and to prepare our environment for the gifts of the divine.

I invite each of you to come up to the altar, light a white candle, and silently invite the light of God to illuminate these proceedings.

Be the first to start. Step up to altar, close your eyes for five to ten seconds as you make your silent prayer, then light candle with match. Gesture to next person to come up to altar. When all white candles are lit, ring bell to signal the end of this ritual. Pick up blank book from altar and read the following out loud.

This book represents the book of my life with _____ *[former spouse]*. I would like you to help me close it. I have written a few thoughts on what our marriage was like, the light and dark sides. Feel free to read them, then write your own thoughts on what made us a good pair or not so good for each other. You can keep it brief; we're not writing a book, just its final sentences! It can be as simple as "they were good together for a while, but it was time for it to end" or "they had grown apart" or "he was a great guy but not right for her," "he or she could have been more _____ or done more _____." You can write why you thought it should end; you can say you thought I messed it up, or that he did. It doesn't matter; I won't read it. This is our message to the universe that we accept this relationship for what it was—its good sides and its bad—and recognize the wisdom of its coming to a close.

As we do this, I would like each one of us to share a story of a relationship that ended, how we dealt with it, what we learned from it in retrospect. Any advice you'd like to give to the group or to me would also be appreciated. I would be happy to start.

Invite someone up to the altar to write in the book, then begin sharing your thoughts, keeping it brief, then go around the room until everyone has had a turn both at writing in the book and telling her own story. Go up to the altar.

The celestial bodies, or seven planets, have long been associated with various types of magical needs. Saturn is said to rule all matters having to do with endings and over the color black. Planetary angels also rule the planetary bodies. According to a revered treatise on planetary magic, the angel of Saturn is Aratron. On this piece of black paper, I have drawn the symbol for Saturn and the seal of Aratron.* I will wrap the book of my life with _____ *[former spouse]* with this cover, which shall represent the power of Saturn to make the end of my marriage to him smooth, healthy, and liberating. I will seal it with tape, then tie it with rope, while asking the angel Aratron to watch over me as I turn the last page of this book and close it forever.

I am going to pass this sealed book around the room. As you hold it in your hands, take a moment also to hold it to your heart as you make a silent prayer to Aratron to help me see this process through. Your loving wish that this comes to pass, plus that of Saturn overseen by Aratron, should make this a sure bet! Remember that the key words around this particular ending are smooth, healthy, and liberating!

When everyone is done, say the following out loud.

---

* From *The Complete Book of Amulets & Talismans* by Migene Gonzalez-Wippler

I am going to use this box as a symbol of my marriage to
_____ [former spouse], which is now over. He's lucky I
didn't choose a coffin!!! [Show that you are placing book in
box.] I am going to put these items in the box, each of them
symbols of our former marriage.

> As you do this, explain each of the items that represent the
> beginning and ending of the relationship, as suggested in
> Pre-ceremony Preparations list. Close box and put it to the
> side. Later you can stow box away or keep it within view for
> as long as you need to. It represents the end of your mar-
> riage and your acceptance of this fact. Ring the bell to sig-
> nal the end of this ritual.

HERBS, FLOWERS, PLANTS, AND TREES

The gifts that Mother Nature has bestowed upon us—her
herbs, flowers, plants, and trees—are there to remind us of
our connection to the earth. The life force that exists in
human beings brings us the magic of breath. The life force
within green, growing things serves to nourish, revitalize,
heal, and intoxicate us while bringing home our interdependent nature with Mother Earth. Endless numbers of
books have been written on the medicinal and magical properties of herbs, flowers, and trees. We use herbs and spices
fully thankful for their wonderful attributes and for their
power to bring these gifts into our lives. [Pick up bowl with
herb mix.] This bowl is filled with simple vegetable oil to
which I added a mix of herbs easily found in most kitchens:
chili powder, cinnamon, and ginger. They each have magical
properties of their own, but together they make a powerful
combination for rituals that entail literally "taking your life
back!"* Now, I want to tell you a little about color.

*From *Everyday Magic* by Dorothy Morrison

COLOR

Color is one of the properties of light. Dating back as far as 3000 B.C., astrologers, astronomers, and philosophers believed that colors give off vibrations, each of which is ruled by one of the seven planets. In turn, seven planetary angels rule these planets. Science has proven that the human brain emits visible color vibrations known as the aura, which, when studied, can give great insight into a person's character.

The vibration given off by each color plays a large part in the physical world. It affects our decisions, our energy and productivity levels as well as the way we feel and act. The use of colors in ceremony serves to summon the forces and attributes of the planets and angels associated with them.

Now I will pass around these candles one at a time. They have been chosen for their colors. I will tell you *[point to first person]* the significance of each color first, hand it to you, and ask you to dip your hand in the bowl. Rub this potent oil all over the candle or anoint it, then pass the candle on to the next person. When you do so, also tell the next person the meaning of the color in question. The reason I won't say the properties of the colors out loud is to avoid disturbing the concentration in the room. As you anoint the candle, concentrate on your wish and prayer that I succeed in taking my life back with a minimum amount of drama—that is to say, in a smooth and easy-going way. All of your combined energies, along with the power of these herbs and color rays will ensure success. When the candle makes its way back to me, I will do the same, and then set it on this plate. When all the candles have been anointed, as we all visualize the goal, I will light them. Remember the power of our intention can make anything happen!

To keep things moving, hand a different colored candle to the two people at the beginning and end of the circle (or opposite ends of the room).

These colors are associated with the following properties:

Red	Taking control of difficult situations, strength
Green	Independence, facing up to challenges
Mauve	Self-confidence, conviction
Gold	Security
Teal	Expansion
Silver	Peace from inner chaos
Pink	Harmony
Yellow	Joy

When all candles are set down on plate, bring everyone's attention to the front of the room and to you by reading the following out loud.

I will light the candles now. As I do so, please close your eyes and imagine a strong, independent, secure, open, and happy me *[or divorcée's name]* taking back my life. You can do this however you please. You can picture me flexing my muscles in your mind's eye, or you can see me walking down the street with a determined step. You can imagine me swimming hearty laps in the ocean or negotiating the purchase of a house or car without hesitation. You get the picture, I think.

Light the candles, close your eyes, and visualize. After a few moments, ring the bell to signal the end of this ritual.

At the beginning of this ceremony, we closed the book on my marriage to _____ *[spouse's name]*. Now we will write the book of my new life. I am going to hand out a white sheet of paper to each of you, and even though you may or may not have any drawing abilities, I am going to ask you to draw any imagery that says growth, blossoming, blooming, leaping, flying, or soaring. The obvious images are plants, trees, flowers, and birds. But you can get as creative as you like: speeding bullets, cars, or animals! It's up to you. It is perfectly okay to draw stick figures. It can be a really bad drawing! This is not a contest. It's supposed to be fun, or even funny. Feel free to give your drawing an explanation like _____ [divorcée's name] blooms like a spring flower or this tree represents _____ [divorcée's name] reaching for the sky.

These two pieces of cardboard will function as the book's front and back covers. In this bowl is a "new beginning" herb formula. It is a mix of frankincense, lemon peel, and myrrh. These herbs are used for healing and achieving wellness and happiness as well as for calling upon God. This bowl of honey which represents a sweeter life. When you have finished your drawing, dip this paintbrush into the honey, brush a smear of it on the book's front cover, then take a pinch from the herbs and sprinkle it on. When everyone is done, I will wrap the cover with some plastic wrap and tape it closed. I've punched three holes into the white sheets of paper, as well as the front and back cover. I will use [string, rope, whatever you decide to use] to tie it all together. Having this new book will enable me to keep your support, encouragement, and love with me always. I will also add blank sheets of paper so that I can continue to create drawings of hope and expansion whenever I need the inspiration.

Before we begin, though, I would like to call on Papa Legba, Haitian spirit of the crossroads, who opens doorways to opportunity and who facilitates communication:

Papa Legba, please honor us with your presence and bless us with the gift of opportunity as we all begin our lives again and again with each new day.

Hand out sheets of paper and begin drawing. When everyone has completed her drawing, bind drawings together into a book, as indicated. Ring bell to signal the end of this ritual.

Thank you all so much. If you'll excuse me for a moment, I'm going to change into my new, fabulous, single woman clothes! I chose to wear black because it represents endings and separation; and I've chosen to enter my new life in red, which represents success, vitality, energy, and passion!

When you emerge, everyone will probably applaud. Take a bow; acknowledge your friends' love.

[Walk to altar, point to plant on floor or side table, lift pitcher of water] This plant represents _____ *[former spouse].* I shower you with spring water in the hope that you will grow, prosper, and flourish in your new life. *[He's lucky I chose water!!!]*

Water plant, which you can later present to your former spouse as an offering, or you may keep it or dispose of it as you wish. Bring out tray of wine or champagne glasses, fill them, and serve your friends.

I would like to offer a toast to you, my friends, whose loving energy, support, and presence in this room fill me with gratitude and inspiration. I can't ever thank you enough. I also want to offer a toast to the spirits of nature, the angels and deities whose assistance I carry with me from this day forward. And finally, I would like for us to raise our glasses to new beginnings!

END OF CEREMONY

MENOPAUSE

Celebrating Freedom and Wisdom

INTRODUCTION

As I sit down to write this introduction, I am recuperating from a very, very hot flash. I can't do it, I say to myself. I hate these things. They make me crazy. They piss me off. They feel like an obnoxious invasion of my body. During certain periods of time, they interrupt my sleep at night, sometimes up to three times, making me cranky and irritable the next day. What am I going to tell people? Honor your hot flashes? Celebrate your wrinkles and graying hair? I feel like a fraud. I won't do it, I say to myself, I'm just not ready. I'm just being honest with myself. I'll replace this ceremony with another one. And then this quiet voice intrudes, whispering, "Maybe you really need to do a ceremony around this. Maybe it will help." And somehow, I know it's true.

When I was in my thirties, I used to swear that I would grow old gracefully. "I'll never color my hair!" I declared to friends and myself. And then the gray started to arrive—not in a lovely salt-and-pepper pattern like some of my more fortunate friends, just along the crown. And still I persevered. But more and more, people were asking why I looked so tired. One day, after denying fatigue one time too many, I thought to hell with this! I marched down to the closest drug store and purchased a package of hair color. I won't bore you with the trials and tribulations of trying to match colors, damaged hair, five-hour stints, and so much money spent at hair salons, etc. Growing old gracefully is turning out to be a lot more challenging than I imagined! So here comes that recurring phenomenon: transition. It's always challenging, often difficult. It's also a standard test of patience and acceptance, courtesy of the universe.

Really, this isn't much different than dealing with the pain of growing out a very short or very bad haircut. It's going to be tough for a while, as your mirror tells you on a daily basis that you look funny and weird. But you know that if you can just hang in there for a while, your natural self will eventually emerge—hopefully a little bit more patient and accepting of life. As our life cycles change, we can also look forward to the flowering of all the wisdom we've acquired throughout the years—wisdom in the realms of beauty, sexuality, spirituality, and in the realm of our senses.

Any rite-of-passage ceremony—especially for this particular rite of passage is designed to help us develop the following essential elements:

❧ Patience

❧ Acknowledgement of certain inevitabilities

❧ Acceptance of who we are at all stages of our lives

A very wise teacher of mine once said that the only thing you can count on is change. If things are going terribly, he said, just wait. It will change. And if things are going great, just wait. It will change. That is the nature of life. We can rail against it. We can wish it was different, but it wouldn't help. All we can do is accept it and enjoy as best we can until we turn that corner. That's what I'm going to try to remember next time I have a hot flash. Accept it— they only last about three minutes, after all—then I can really enjoy that feeling of having turned the corner.

PRE-CEREMONY PREPARATIONS

Ask everyone to come prepared to share an inspiring story of the end of something (a relationship, friendship, an era, a way of thinking, a way of being or looking) that was a challenge. It should be about a challenge that they made peace with.

Prepare a designated chair for the subject of the ceremony. It might be most convenient to place your guest on your right or left, and the altar on the other side. This way you will have access to all necessary items on the altar and your guest will be in a prime position at the head of the room.

Place eleven white candles around the room to create a circle around the group. They may be placed on tables, mantels, chairs, and/or the floor.

Choose a spot or table for the altar. Lay out these items, as follows:

- One bell

- Charcoal blocks (the kind used for burning incense, not barbecuing) and tweezers or tongs for handling charcoal

- Dried rosemary herbs

- Heat-resistant plate or saucer

- Matches

- Yellow cotton cloth (big enough to be tied around the neck and used as a cape)

- Eight small-to-medium cans of paint (water-based acrylic or oil, doesn't matter) in following colors: red, green, mauve, gold, pink, teal, dark blue, silver

- Eight small-to-medium paint brushes

- Four pitchers—one filled with milk, one with water, one with water plus red vegetable dye to make it red, one empty.

- One small-to-medium plant (use backyard or front yard instead, if available)

REMINDER: *Please remember to read through the ceremony in its entirety so that you can make appropriate changes. Practice reading it out loud in order to familiarize yourself and become comfortable with it. Most importantly, if the way I have written it does not feel suitable for you, or in keeping with the way you would normally express yourself, simply use it as a guideline for your own words where needed.*

PLEASE NOTE: All sections of the ceremony are meant to be read out loud, except for instructions set in italics.

MENOPAUSE
Celebrating Freedom and Wisdom

WELCOME

Welcome, everyone. This ceremony has been conceived with love, and it is assumed that everyone here comes with wishes of love and well-being for _____ *[special guest]*.

[Special guest] _____ is entering a very special phase in her life, one that can be filled with self-doubt and worry over the many endings and changes that come with it: the end of her empowering monthly bleeding; the end of her child-bearing capacities; the changes in her appearance, and the puzzlement that hormones can wreak—like the time-worn question, is it hot in here or is it me? But every negative has its positive: on the other side of gloom comes the glow of illumination; because of fear we know relief; and being in the gutter can change simply by looking up at the stars. So along with those often challenging and distressing issues comes the vital dawning of a new era in a woman's life—an era often demeaned primarily because we hang on to the past, refusing to look forward to see what's next. The adventure continues, it turns out, ever sprouting each new life phase. This cycle of a woman's life holds the promise of transcendence, the pinnacle of spiritual growth. It is the high point of womanhood. It is a time for achievement, an excellent time to manifest dreams and to enjoy the body in new, stimulating ways. We are collectors of wisdom as we negotiate sisterhood, motherhood, and femaleness. The word "woman" evokes all that is sensual, sensitive, knowing. It speaks to what is nurturing, nourishing, and life-giving. A

woman is creator, provider, healer, warrior. This new phase represents the flowering of all these powers, transforming you into a natural teacher and true appreciator of life's treasures. You are now free to be the original bon vivant! This is your time. Take this life with gusto. Today's ceremony is meant to get you on your way.

CEREMONY

The stringing together of certain rituals performed with special intent is called ceremony. Ceremonies are important because they serve to gather up all of our energies and to focus them on one specific thing in this case, helping to make _____ 's *[special guest]* transition into the age of wisdom as smooth and graceful as possible. Choosing a predetermined time, place, and setting for an event; using symbolic words, aromas, sounds, and actions; and adding the participation of special people has the effect of lifting us out of our everyday frame of reference. We suddenly find ourselves transported into the realm of the extraordinary, where anything and everything is possible simply because we wish it to be. Though some of the things we do today may seem unusual, know that they have all been carefully researched in the hope of recreating centuries-old practices from various corners of the world—rituals that serve to harness the positive power of the saints, spirits, angels, gods, and goddesses that surround us, and to make our desires known to them. As you know, if you don't ask, you won't receive.

To begin this ceremony, I would like to call on certain goddesses. I ask them to reinforce the power generated among us here today, to instill in us their ancient knowledge, to share with us their mysterious ways and to bless us with their divine presence. But before invoking these special feminine spirits, I would like to come around the room with some rosemary herbs.

HERBS, FLOWERS, PLANTS, AND TREES

The gifts that Mother Nature has bestowed upon us—her herbs, flowers, plants, and trees—are there to remind us of our connection to the earth. The life force that exists in human beings brings us the magic of breath. The life force within green, growing things serves to nourish, revitalize, heal, and intoxicate us while bringing home our interdependent nature with Mother Earth. Endless numbers of books have been written on the medicinal and magical properties of herbs, flowers, and trees. We use rosemary and charcoal here, fully thankful for their wonderful attributes and for their power to bring these gifts into our lives.

When rosemary is burned, it releases great waves of purifying energy. Like sage, it is used to drive negativity out; and when smoldered on charcoal, herbal lore teaches that it helps in the receipt of knowledge. I will light this charcoal block now. When I come around you, take just two or three of these spiky rosemary leaves at a time, and place them onto the charcoal. Take in a nice, deep breath, and invite any worries, concerns, fears, or stress to flow on out of this room. This will leave you open to receive the wisdom of this day.

Start by lighting charcoal. To light it, hold the block with tweezers or tongs; light match and hold flame to the edge of block until you see sparks, which means it is ready, or hot enough. Set it down on a small heat-resistant plate or saucer. Be the first to place rosemary leaves onto the charcoal. Take in a whiff of the smoke, and close your eyes for a moment. Visualize your worries leaving through an open window or door. You should take no more than fifteen to twenty seconds during visualization in order to keep things moving. Begin with your special guest, and then go around the room. When everyone has had a turn, ring bell to signal the end of this ritual.

The feminine nature of the great mystery referred to as God is ever-present with us as we go about our daily lives. Today we call upon just a special few manifestations of the goddess as she is known and revered throughout the world.

There are eleven candles placed around the room. After each goddess is named, I will call on the person nearest to each candle to light it.

CANDLES

Ever since primitive humans discovered that fire kept them warm and dry and made their food taste better, they went to great extremes to safeguard it from the elements. In fire they also saw a resemblance to the sun, whose rays provided them with warmth, and with light, which allowed them to face their enemies without fear. In this way the sun and fire came to be worshiped as gods of protection from evil influences and spirits and as gods of light, warmth, and healing. It is easy to see how these beliefs gave way to the practice of candle burning as invitation for the light of God to come into a human heart, to purify and cleanse the environment, to protect, and to take away the darkness.

A heartfelt belief in any one thing becomes reality for the believer. Centuries of belief in fire and the sun as beneficent gods have made them such. Passed on to modern humans from generation to generation, instinctively we light candles today for the same reasons. In the home, candles are burned to create warmth, to generate beautiful light, and to transform the environment—all of which have roots in the primal urges experienced by our ancestors. In ceremony, we burn candles in the hope of consciously recreating these now deeply rooted beliefs in the power of fire to bring us closer to the light, to help us attain enlightenment, and to prepare our environment for the gifts of the divine.

INVOCATION

So, today we invoke:

- Mother Earth, you who have given birth to our planet and the nature that surrounds us, we ask that you come and be with us today, in this room. We ask that you give us of your nourishment and specifically, that you hold our dearest friend _____ *[special guest]* to your breast. Please wrap her in your abundant arms and give her a special dose of comfort, love, and sustenance as she makes her way forward in her next life phase.

- Yemaya, you who are considered mother of all human beings by West African and Afro-Caribbean peoples, please imbue _____ *[special guest]* with your grace and spiciness and knowledge of female mysteries. As a goddess of power and possibilities, we thank you for whatever opportunities you may present to _____ *[special guest]* and for the power you give her to pursue them.

- Changing Woman, Navajo deity who has been likened to the ever-changing moon, goddess of transformation who brings long life and the ability to transform oneself from baby to girl and back to woman at will, we ask that you help make _____ 's *[special guest]* change from fabulous woman to fabulous goddess of wisdom a smooth and stress-free journey.

- Tara, Hindu and Buddhist goddess of compassion, eternal light, and life, please come so that we may be reminded of the fleeting nature of our strongest emotions. With your third eye and the eyes you reflect in your hands and feet, help us and _____ *[special guest]* in particular to see the perfection in each moment.

- Lucina, Roman goddess of the sun and spring, symbol of rebirth, we invite you here today.

❧ Hathor, Egyptian goddess of love, joy, passion, and merriment, please bless _____ [special guest] with your infectious zest for life.

❧ Epona, Celtic goddess who represents wild freedom, please unlock the door to _____'s [special guest] most spontaneous urges.

❧ Hecate, Greek goddess of the crossroads, who oversees all of life's passages, please light the way to all the opportunities that await _____ [special guest].

❧ Benten, Japanese goddess of good fortune, prosperity, creativity, and romance, we ask that you please bless _____ [special guest] with your gifts.

❧ Freya, Norse goddess of sexuality, please endow _____ [special guest] with your ancient knowledge of the body and of the ways of pleasure.

❧ And finally, dear Lady of the Moon, recognized in many cultures as the feminine aspect of God, please join us today, bathing us all with the glow of your regenerative and inspiring ways. We honor and embrace you and respectfully ask that you fill our dear friend _____ [special guest] with your innate ability to create new life. [Ring bell to signal end of invocation.]

❀

We allow the future to take shape and texture only when we are able to let go of the past. Now we will help _____ [special guest] surrender to the universe those elements that can now be considered part of her past. There aren't too many of them, but they are significant. We can safely say that with menopause comes the end of these three things:

Bearing children	This ending means that you can no longer regenerate yourself by giving birth to another human being. Regeneration of yourself by re-creating your life is the way to go now!
Producing breast milk	Nourish the people you love with your grace, your spirit, your kindness, your support, and your good intentions. These are your tools now. Use them carefully. They are powerful, as your years on this earth have prepared them for expert use.
Bleeding every month	Since your First Blood, you have experienced monthly physical proof of your divinity as a potential giver of life. The visible connection to your higher self no longer comes because the universe deems it unnecessary. You don't need to be reminded because knowledge of your divinity is closer now, and more obvious. Enjoy the knowing, and accept the responsibility of reminding us all!

Letting go of these three capacities is top priority because they are inextricably tied to so many of the physical and emotional sensations that now come into play. Here I have four pitchers. One is empty and the others contain one of the following:

☞ Water, as a symbol for life, because like life, it flows. Think of this water as _____'s *[special guest]* former capacity to give life through childbirth.

🕭 Milk. Think of this milk as a symbol of _____'s *[special guest]* former ability to produce breast milk.

🕭 Blood. I have added a red vegetable dye to this water in order to symbolize _____'s *[special guest]* former ability to bleed every month.

I would like _____ *[special guest]* to come up to the altar and pour a little bit of liquid from all three pitchers into this empty one. As you do this, visualize each pouring as an offering back to the universe those gifts, which were offered to you so many years ago. When you are done, I would like everyone to come up and do the same. These gifts belong to you, but we are all here to help you surrender them back to the earth.

Motion for special guest to come up and begin. Be the first after her, and then invite each person, one after the other, to come up to the altar for this ritual. When everyone has had a turn, pick up fourth pitcher, which is now filled, and hand it to special guest. Gesture to nearby plant, or ask everyone to follow you out to backyard or front yard, if available.

This plant *[soil, if in yard]* represents the earth from which you came. We invite you to pour the contents of the pitcher back into the earth. This is your way of signaling to the universe your willingness to surrender the _____ *[special guest]* with whom you have been so familiar and to embrace the _____ *[special guest]* who is now in the process of transitioning to a higher place.

Once this is done, ring bell to signal the end of this ritual.

SHARING HISTORY

The power of the spoken word is great. Because we speak and use our voices every day, the power of our words can become diluted. However, when words are spoken with consciousness and intention, there is no limit to the string of actions and reactions they can unleash. This is where the old saying about being careful what you wish for comes from. With that in mind, I asked everyone to come prepared to share a brief story of a time in her life when she faced a challenge or an ending—an ending that was overcome or resolved through acceptance, a welcoming, or an opening of some sort. We want to share stories of coming to terms or making peace with a situation in a way that was inspiring. All of our stories, accumulated on top of each other, will become a tapestry of inspiration woven for _____ *[special guest]* as she faces her own challenges. Unwritten words can be very, very potent in that their echoes reverberate in our memories forever. This is how oral histories are made.

Bear in mind that the stories don't necessarily have to revolve around change-of-life challenges. Your story could be about your first boyfriend, the end of a friendship or relationship, or dealing with a bad haircut or hair coloring. The theme we're going for is acceptance. There's letting go and then there's acceptance. And without acceptance, it is impossible to move on.

Be the first to begin, and then call on each person as you go around the room. When everyone has had a turn, face special guest and say the following out loud.

Dearest _____ *[special guest]*, we call upon the goddesses, who bless us with their presence on this day, to grant you the gifts of acceptance, openness, joy, and zest as you take on this brand new beginning!

Ring bell to signal the end of this ritual. Read the following out loud while facing special guest.

Letting go of the old and accepting what cannot be changed are the first two steps one has to take in order to move forward. Moving forward may be the last and most challenging step. Moving forward requires momentum, strength, vitality, and self-confidence as well as trust that all the cycles of our lives have a purpose. The rituals we've partaken in so far have hopefully provided the momentum. We endeavor now to give you the rest.

CLOAK OF COURAGE

We will now create your Cloak of Courage. I chose this yellow cloth because yellow is the color of joy and success.

COLOR

Color is one of the properties of light. Dating back as far as 3000 B.C., astrologers, astronomers, and philosophers believed that colors give off vibrations, each of which is ruled by one of the seven planets. In turn, seven planetary angels rule these planets. Science has proven that the human brain emits visible color vibrations known as the aura, which, when studied, can give great insight into a person's character.

The vibration given off by each color plays a large part in the physical world. It affects the way we feel and act, our decisions, our energy and productivity levels. The use of colors in ceremony serves to summon the forces and attributes of the planets and angels associated with them.

There are eight cans of paint here, which were specifically chosen for their colors. I will wrap this yellow cloth around _____ *[special guest]* like a cape, then ask all of you to come up one at a time. Please dip a paintbrush into the first can and paint a swath anywhere you like on the cloth. I will start first, telling you the meaning of each color as I go. As you make your mark on the cloak, repeat the words that I say. Your wish and intention is what counts. Remember that a true wish, followed by spoken words, must come true.

Begin first by dipping your brush in red paint can. Read the following aloud.

Red is the color of strength, vitality, and energy. *[Paint swath of color on cloak.]*

Dear _____ *[special guest]*, I wish you strength, vitality, and energy.

Invite next person to come up and do the same, then next person, and so on. When last person is done, move to can of green paint and proceed as before.

Green is the color that governs independence, growth, acceptance of challenges, and prosperity. *[Paint swath of color on cloak.]*

Dear _____ *[special guest]*, I wish you independence, growth, acceptance of challenges and prosperity.

Teal is the color of expansion. *[Repeat as above—I wish you expansion.]*

Mauve is the color of self-confidence and self-trust. *[Repeat as above—I wish you self-confidence and self-trust.]*

Silver is for inner peace. *[Repeat as above—I wish you inner peace.]*

Gold is for security. *[Repeat as above—I wish you security.]*

Pink is for stimulating self-love. *[Repeat as above—I wish you self-love.]*

Dark blue is for invoking feminine deities. *[Repeat as above— Call them when you need them!]*

When everyone has painted a stroke of color on the cloak, ring bell to signal end of this ritual. Face guest of honor and read the following out loud:

Dear _____ *[special guest]*, take this Cloak of Courage with our love, support, and best intentions. Whenever you feel you need it, throw it over your shoulders, cover yourself with it in bed or when you watch TV, or pull it out and just look at it! It carries all of our energies, the vibration of this day and of this ceremony. Whenever you touch it or look at it, know that we will be with you.

We revere you, your wisdom, and the spiritual knowledge that you carry. We look to you as our guide and our friend, and we honor the natural healing and intuitive powers that you hold.

Welcome to you, _____ *[special guest]*.

Lead everyone in a round of applause. Propose a toast! Drink wine, champagne, or whatever feels right to celebrate the moment.

END OF CEREMONY

PASSING ONWARD

Making Peace with Death

INTRODUCTION

"If you do not merit death, Gédé will refuse it." That's what Haitian people say about Haitian folklore's Spirit of Death.* They believe Gédé is the lord of death as well as life because it is his job to oversee the cycle of regeneration. He is wise above all other spirits, he is the repository of all the knowledge of the dead, and he wields immense power. He is also sexy, funny, and a real party animal. Being in his company is considered an honor.

Death is that most awesome of events because it represents our final act on this earth—the last breath, last wish, last word, last moment. But in many, many cultures, death is just the beginning of our soul's journey to the next phase of growth and transformation—two widely sought goals for those of us remaining in life.

Loss can never be light, and grieving can never feel good. The aim of performing a ceremony around the loss of someone we love is not to feel good necessarily. The goal is to formally acknowledge the loss, the sudden lack, the absence; to experience the immensity of it with people who loved the departed soul; to gather the strength needed to help that soul move on into her next life phase; and to use that strength to propel us forward into our own next phase.

Motion represents activity—in this case, the active moving ahead of a soul no longer hampered by a physical body and our own progress as we travel that road to closure, release, and revelation. This ceremony is meant to help embrace that motion.

* According to Donald J. Cosentino in *Vodou: Visions & Voices of Haiti* by Phyllis Galembo

PRE-CEREMONY PREPARATIONS

Ask participants to come prepared to share a story or anecdote about the departed. Stories should be about interactions, significant moments —even difficult ones if they illustrate something meaningful—funny stories, etc.

- White candles (as many as there are participants, plus yourself and the departed)

- Plate large enough to hold all lit candles

- Matches

- Bowl filled with any vegetable oil (preferably not olive) and several drops of sandalwood and lavender essential oils (approximately four to six drops each)

- Spray bottle filled with spring water and several drops of peppermint essential oil

- Designate a chair for the departed. If you feel inclined to decorate it or dress it up with fabric and/or pillows to make it special or throne like, feel free.

- White tablecloth (for altar)

Prepare altar by laying out in an eye-pleasing arrangement things that the departed liked (certain snacks, favorite book, glass of wine, etc.), items that belonged to her (jewelry, perfume, hair ornaments, etc.) and other symbolic objects, such as:
- White flowers

- Photograph of departed

- Photo or representation of deity she might have had an affection for or affiliation with

❧ Actual cross or photo or drawing of a cross to represent the cross-roads, or crossing over from the physical into the metaphysical

❧ Depictions of the moon, stars, heavens

❧ Henna powder or leaves in a bowl (to help departed make his/her journey into the afterlife) and for the healing process of friends and family

❧ Prepare a meal and drinks for later consumption by participants. It should be made up of foods that departed liked.

REMINDER: *Please remember to read through the ceremony in its entirety so that you can make appropriate changes. Practice reading it out loud in order to familiarize yourself and become comfortable with it. Most importantly, if the way I have written it does not feel suitable for you, or in keeping with the way you would normally express yourself, simply use it as a guideline for your own words where needed. For simplicity's sake, I use "her" or "she" throughout the ceremony rather than the more cumbersome "he/she" or "him/her." Please replace it with the proper pronoun where appropriate.*

PLEASE NOTE: All sections of the ceremony are meant to be read out loud, except for instructions set in italics.

PASSING ONWARD
Making Peace with Death

WELCOME

Welcome, everyone. We are here today to love _____ *[departed's name]* one more time. When someone dies, people begin using the past tense when referring to them. That makes sense, but for me, it never felt right to say "I or he or she loved her. We still love _____ *[departed]* and will continue to do so for a long time. But today, we want to love her in the BIGGEST possible way, which is to give her our blessing to move forward in her path toward growth, evolution, and regeneration. And we want to do this in style!

By the same token, we are also here to love ourselves, to acknowledge the deep feelings of loss and hurt and pain that come with having to let go of someone who meant so much to us; and to ask that she watch over us as we move on in our next life phase without her physical presence. We are here to give our love, support and encouragement to _____ *[relatives]*, who will miss _____ *[departed]* most of all. We are also here to reconsider death. Maybe it isn't the final period after multiple pages of sentences filled with colors, emotions, and sounds. Perhaps it is the first word in the best sequel ever written. A sequel in which the soul departs to new, mysterious, and exotic lands while we embark on our own new journey of discovery. Of course, there's no getting around the fact that *we* don't have new landscapes or exotic destinations in our immediate future. We have a lot of cleaning up to do first—taking care of the gear she didn't take because it would have been too cumbersome, deciding how to make the best use of the empty space her leaving created, dealing with some of the anger we might feel about all that extra work, and just plain missing her.

So we come together today to accomplish four things: to acknowledge the absence of _____ [departed] in our lives; to do some of that hard work, cleaning up; to give her a great send-off; and to honor and embrace the forever shifting story that is this life—our life. A ceremony performed around the event of someone's death isn't necessarily designed to make us feel good. It is designed to make us feel at peace.

CEREMONY

The stringing together of certain rituals performed with special intent is called ceremony. Ceremonies are important because they serve to gather up all of our energies and to focus them on one specific thing, in this case, two things— the acceptance of _____'s [departed] departure to new realms, and the peace we seek as we move forward toward our own destinies. Choosing a pre-determined time, place, and setting for an event; using symbolic words, aromas, sounds, and actions; and adding the participation of special people has the effect of lifting us out of our everyday frame of reference into the realm of the extraordinary, where anything and everything is possible simply because we wish it to be. Though some of the things we do today may seem unusual, know that they have all been carefully researched in the hopes of recreating centuries-old practices from various corners of the world. These rituals serve to harness the positive power of the saints, spirits, angels, gods, and goddesses that surround us, and to make our will known to them. As you know, if you don't ask, you won't receive.

BELL

I am going to start the ceremony by ringing this bell around the perimeter of the room. Three thousand years ago, in recognizing that everything in creation was imbued with a life force or energy, the ancient Chinese started practicing Feng

Shui *[pronounced Feng Shway]* as a practical means of redirecting the flow of energy in a space. It created powerful adjustments that efficiently changed the course of their life. Today Feng Shui is widely accepted as a natural way to attune oneself with the elements in order to harmonize, balance, and enhance the flow and level of energy in one's environment. The use of bells is prevalent in Feng Shui practices primarily to purify a space, disperse static energy, and to create a sacred circle of sound whose vibration and movement will ward off negative spirits and attract the angels. I use the bell here today for the same purpose and invite you to listen to its tone, allowing it to fill your being as you experience your energy vibrate at a new, heightened level.

Walk slowly around perimeter of the room as you ring the bell. Repeat as many times as you wish until you feel a change or clearing of the vibration in the room. Once around the room is usually enough.

Now I will spray this mix of spring water and peppermint oil into the air and around you.

HERBS, FLOWERS, PLANTS, AND TREES

The gifts that Mother Nature has bestowed upon us—her flowers, plants, trees and herbs—are here to remind us of our connection to the earth. Just as the life force that exists in human beings brings us the magic of breath, so the life force within green, growing things serves to nourish, revitalize, heal, and intoxicate us while bringing home our interdependent nature with Mother Earth. Endless numbers of books have been written on the medicinal and magical properties of herbs, flowers, and trees and we use them here, fully thankful for their wonderful attributes and for their power to bring these gifts into our lives. Peppermint is known to have wonderful healing and purification properties. Its presence will further raise the vibration of the room, and sprayed around each of you, will help start the healing process.

Go around the room, spraying into the air, into corners and toward the ceiling. Then go to each participant and spray around her.

This table is our dedicated altar space today. An altar is traditionally considered a special place where human beings can meet with God, the divine, that Great Mystery, or whatever term you use for the sacred. It is a place to make offerings to deities whose favors and help you want to formally request. It is also an area designated to reflect the elements and intent of any given ceremony. *[Point to chair designated as the departed's seat.]* This chair is for _____ *[departed]*. We would like her presence here today, so I am going to ask each of you to take turns coming up to the altar, placing a candle on this plate and lighting it. Later, when you leave, please remember to take a candle home with you. You can light it every day until it burns down or you can keep it and light it whenever you miss _____ *[departed]* or want to feel her presence.

CANDLES

Ever since primitive humans discovered that fire kept them warm and dry and made their food taste better, they went to great extremes to safeguard it from the elements. In fire they also saw a resemblance to the sun, whose rays provided them with warmth, and with light, which allowed them to face their enemies without fear. In this way the sun and fire came to be worshiped as gods of protection from evil influences and spirits and as gods of light, warmth, and healing. It is easy to see how these beliefs gave way to the practice of candle burning as invitation for the light of God to come into a human heart, to purify and cleanse the environment, to protect, and to take away the darkness.

A heartfelt belief in any one thing becomes reality for the believer. Centuries of heartfelt belief in fire and the sun as beneficent gods have made them such. Passed on to modern humans from generation to generation, instinctively we light candles today for the same reasons. In the home, candles are burned to create warmth, to generate beautiful light, and to transform the environment—all of which have roots in the primal urges experienced by our ancestors. In ceremony, we burn candles in the hopes of consciously re-creating these now deeply rooted beliefs in the power of fire to bring us closer to the light, to help us attain enlightenment, and to prepare our environment for the gifts of the divine.

Pick up bowl filled with vegetable, lavender, and sandalwood oils.

This bowl is filled with a mixture of lavender and sandalwood essential oils. When burned, sandalwood generates very high spiritual vibrations, and it is often used for healing purposes. Lavender promotes happiness and peace. The combination of these two herbs has the effect of conjuring spirits! When you come up to the altar, dip your hand in the bowl and anoint [or rub] the candle with it, then light the candle and place it on the plate. As you light your candle, think of it as inviting _____ [departed], whose spirit is now joined with the Light, to visit with us here today and to illuminate these proceedings with her presence.

Serve as example. Hold match to bottom of candle until wax drops onto plate. Set candle down and light it. Stop for a moment to make that silent invitation, and then ask the next person to come up to the altar and do the same. When everyone is done, lift the candle-filled plate from the altar, hold it up toward the designated chair, and say the following out loud:

Dear _____ *[departed]*, we thank you for being with us here today as you have in body so many times before. Our love has brought you here, and we know you can hear us as we remember you with our words and in our hearts and as we acknowledge your passing through the ritual acts we perform in this ceremony.

[Turn to face participants.] I would now like each one of us to share a story about _____ *[departed]* that stands out as particularly wonderful, difficult, poignant, insightful, funny—even things that might have made you mad at her—anything to help us remember her as the fully rounded individual that she was in this life. You may want to talk about your feelings when you first heard of _____'s *[departed]* death—the shock, the grief, the devastation. In African cultures, grief is a public, often boisterous affair because it is believed that only by truly and completely feeling sorrow can we eventually let it go and move on. I don't believe any of us here is a stranger to tears. Tears are a natural outlet for pain. If all you want to do is cry, feel free! If no stories come to mind, you might want to take this opportunity to say to _____ *[departed]* something you wish you'd said to her before she left her body; or what you might say to her now if she were alive. After all, she's right here. *[You might want to gesture to chair.]*

> *When the last person has spoken, ring bell to signal the end of this ritual. Turn toward chair and read the following out loud:*

Dear _____ *[departed]*, we miss you so much. We think of you often and carry you with us in our hearts. We thank the Highest for the knowledge that you are where you need to be—learning, growing, reflecting on your life here on earth, and experiencing the bliss of communion with all that is. We also want you to take a part of us with you and to carry our love with you as you journey to the new beginning that awaits you. *[Turn to the participants.]* Now we will do a very simple but powerful visualization. Please pick a scene or an element of nature and imagine yourself in it fully, incorporating smells, sounds, and the way it feels to be there. Fill your being with that image, making it the purest and highest thought you ever had about yourself, and then offer that image to _____ [departed], so that she may take the beauty of this earth and of your spirit with her wherever she goes. I'll offer a few examples to get us going:

Who am I?

- I am the most beautiful of all gardens.

- I am the brightest of all stars.

- I am the most beautiful of all rivers.

- I am the sweetest smelling red rose.

- I am a jasmine bush in full bloom.

- I am the most lyrical bird.

- I am a moonlit sky.

- I am the warm, blue Caribbean sea.

- I am the red desert sunset.

- I am a pond filled with pink lotus flowers.

- I am a bright blue sunny sky.

You can choose one of these or create your own. Speak who you are out loud, take a moment to see yourself that way, and then offer that gift to _____ [departed]. I will start things off. Feel free to use these simple words:

I am a starry night *[or imagery of your choice. Stop, close your eyes for a moment to let the picture sink into your being, then continue]*

Dear _____ *[departed]*, I offer it to you with all my love.

> *When everyone is done, ring the bell to signal the end of this ritual. Turn to chair.*

Dear _____ *[departed]*, we thank you for blessing us with your beautiful spirit today. Your crossing over to the other side is a reminder of our own mortality, the inevitability of life's natural cycle. Though we may try to embrace the reality of your death, it will probably be easier for us to try embracing our mortality; to begin making friends with it, accepting it as gently as summer becoming fall; and to do all we can to move forward as gracefully as possible into a life without you. We say good-bye to you now and welcome your spirit in our dreams and in our waking life. We'll be looking for your tips and signposts along the way, whenever you think we need help. May your voyage be blessed with love, beauty, grace, and easy choices.

> *Lead everyone in applause as spirit departs. When applause is over, turn to participants. If you are at the departed's home and have arranged to help her relative[s] clear out her belongings, packing boxes, etc., now would be the time to lead the group into that part of the ceremony.*

Earlier I mentioned space clearing, the mental and emotional element of cleaning out the upheaval that death often leaves in its wake. But there is also the actual, physical stuff too! And as you know, _____ *[departed's relative]* could use some help in boxing up and clearing out _____ 's *[departed]* belongings. This is the time for us to lend our support in a very grounded and practical way. *[Turn to relative.]* Show us the way!

If actual, physical space clearing is not going to happen as part of the ceremony, plan to do something physical, which will symbolize clearing away the debris that death leaves behind. This can include:

᰸ *Planting seeds in a garden or individual planters*

᰸ *Everyone joining together to prepare a meal*

᰸ *Giving each other shoulder or scalp rubs*

᰸ *Going for a walk*

᰸ *Doing yoga*

᰸ *Something physical that the departed would have liked*

Earlier I mentioned space clearing, the mental and emotional element of cleaning out the upheaval that death often leaves in its wake. But usually there is hard, labor intensive work that needs to be done too. Since packing up _____ 's *[departed]* belongings *[is already done, isn't possible, or whatever the reason is]* for the next half hour, we are going to _____, to symbolize the often-physical deeds that must be taken care of in order to move forward.

Ring bell to signal end of this ritual. Read out loud:

I invite you all to share this meal, which is made up of _____ 's *[departed]* favorite dishes. Start the meal with a toast to the departed.

END OF CEREMONY

⚚ RUNES ⚚

ᚠ Prosperity	ᛉ Protection
ᚢ Physical health, vitality	ᛦ Vital energies
ᚦ Willpower	↑ Victory
ᚨ Wisdom	ᛒ Emotional stability
ᚱ Taking control	ᛗ Safe journey
ᚲ Skill, knowledge	ᛞ Self-improvement
ᚷ Union, partnership, agreement	ᛚ Growth
ᚹ Joy, comfort, happiness	ᚷ Invocation of God
ᚻ The unanticipated	ᛞ Breakthrough
ᚾ Self-control	ᛜ Invocation of ancestors
ᛁ Rest	ᛇ Good fortune
ᛃ Change	ᚦ To attract and express lo
ᛈ Metaphysical communication	ᛋ Energy
ᛉ Discover secrets	ᚾ Productive journey

✌ SYMBOL OF SATURN ✌

♄

✌ SEAL OF ARATRON ✌

✄ BIBLIOGRAPHY ✄

❀ **BRONER, E.M.**
Bringing Home the Light
Tulsa, OK, Council Oak Books, 1999, Pages 57-65. Ms

❀ **BUDAPEST, ZSUZSANNA E.**
The Grandmother of Time, A Women's Book of Celebrations,
Spells, and Sacred Objects For Every Month of the Year
San Francisco, CA, Harper & Row, 1989

————————.
The Holy Book of Women's Mysteries, Feminist Witchcraft,
Goddess Rituals, Spellcasting, and Other Womanly Arts.
Berkeley, CA, Wingbow Press, 1989

❀ **CAMACHE, HENRI**
The Master Book of Candle Burning,
How to Burn Candles for Every Purpose
Old Bethpage, NY, Original Publications, 1998

❀ **CUNNINGHAM, SCOTT**
The Complete Book of Incense, Oils & Brews
St. Paul, MN, Llewellyn Publications, 1986
Cunningham's Encyclopedia of Magical Herbs
St. Paul, MN, Llewellyn Publications, 1993

❀ **CUROTT, PHYLLIS**
Book of Shadows, A Modern Woman's Journey into
the Wisdom of Witchcraft and the Magic of the Goddess
New York, NY, Broadway Books, 1998

❀ **DAVID, JUDITHANN H. ,AND J.P. VAN HULLE**
Michael's Gemstone Dictionary
Orinda, CA, Michael Educational Foundation and Affinity Press, 1990

❀ **DRIVER, TOM F.**
The Magic of Ritual, Our Need for Liberating Rites
that Transform Our Lives and Our Communities
New York, NY, Harper, 1991

❀ **DUNWICH, GERINA**
Wicca Candle Magick
Secaucus, NJ, Carol Publishing Group, 1989

❀ **GALEMBO, PHYLLIS**
Vodou, Visions and Voices of Haiti
Berkeley, CA, Ten Speed Press, 1998

❀ **GONZÁLEZ-WIPPLER, MIGENE**
The Complete Book of Amulets & Talismans
St. Paul, MN, Llewellyn Publications, 1998

❀ **JORDON, MICHAEL**
Encyclopedia of Gods, Over 2500 Deities of the World
New York, NY, Facts on File, Inc., 1993

❀ **KINGSTON, KAREN**
*Creating Sacred Space with Feng Shui, Learn the Art
of Space Clearing and Bring New Energy into Your Life*
New York, NY, Broadway Books, 1997

❀ **LEVINE, ELIZABETH RESNICK. ED.**
*A Ceremonies Sampler, New Rites, Celebrations
and Observances of Jewish Women*
San Diego, CA, Woman's Institute for Continuing Jewish Education, 1991

❀ **LIPTAK, KAREN**
Coming of Age, Tradition and Rituals around the World
Brookfield, CN, The Millbook Press, 1994

❀ **MARCINIAK, BARBARA**
Earth, Pleiadian Keys to the Living Library
Santa Fe, NM, Bear & Company Publishing, 1995

❀ **METRICK, SYDNEY BARBARA**
*Crossing the Bridge, Creating Ceremonies for
Grieving and Healing from Life's Losses*
Berkeley, CA, Celestial Arts, 1994

❀ **MORRISON, DOROTHY**
Everyday Magic
Saint Paul, MN, Llewellyn Publications, 1998

❀ **MOUNTAINWATER, SHEKINAH**
A Workbook of Goddess Magic
Freedom, CA, The Crossing Press, 1991

❀ **MOURA, ANN (AOUMIEL)**
Green Witchcraft, Folk Magic, Fairy Lore & Herb Craft
St. Paul, MN, Llewellyn Publications, 1998

✿ **MYERS, J. (with the editors of Hallmark Cards)**
Complete Book of American Holidays
Garden City, NY, Doubleday & Company, 1972

✿ **POLLACK, RACHEL**
The Power of Ritual
The Omega Institute Mind, Body, Spirit Series
NewYork, NY, Dell Books, 2000

✿ **RUSHTON, LUCY**
Birth Customs (Comparing Religions)
New York, NY, Thomson Learning, 1992

✿ **SOMÉ, MALIDOMA PATRICE**
*Of Water and the Spirit, Ritual, Magic and Initiation
in the Life of an African Shaman*
PUBLISHER LOCATION?—SL, Penguin Books, 1994

✿ **STEIN, DIANE**
*The Goddess Book of Days, A Perpetual
366 Day Engagement Calendar*
Freedom, CA, The Crossing Press, 1995

✿ **VALIENTE, DOREEN**
Natural Magic
Custer, WA, Phoenix Publishing, Inc., 1975

✿ **WALKER, BARBARA**
The Woman's Dictionary of Symbols and Sacred Objects
San Francisco,CA, Harper San Francisco, 1988

✿ **WORWOOD, VALERIE ANN**
The Complete Book of Essential Oils & Aromatherapy
San Rafael, CA, New World Library, 1991

✿ **INTERNET**
On numerology: www.wideninghorizons.com
                     www.spiritlink.com
On full moon lore: www.SkepDic.com

❧ INDEX ❧

Carine Fabius was born in Port-au-Prince, Haiti and grew up in New York City where she worked as an assistant editor in the programming division of CBS Television. She moved to Miami at the age of 23, then headed west to Los Angeles where she worked for several years in the public relations field. In 1990, with her husband, Pascal Giacomini, she opened Galerie Lakaye, a Caribbean and Latin art gallery with a focus on Haitian art. Fabius and her husband later opened Lakaye Studio to help introduce the art of temporary tattoos to the United States and began marketing "Earth Henna®" body painting kits. Fabius also creates the Ispiritus line of jewelry.

"I am very interested in connecting with God, or Spirit, or Universal Life Force in whatever way I can, and in whatever form that takes," says Fabius. "Creating and performing ceremonies, along with regular meditation, helps put that goal within reach for me. Over the years I have written and performed many ceremonies for friends looking to infuse their celebratory events with conscious intent, uniqueness and an extra dose of love."

Fabius, also the author of *Mehndi: The Art of Henna Body Painting,* has created kits that provide the components suggested for each ceremony in *Ceremonies for Real Life.* Learn more about these and her henna kits at www.earthhenna.com.

Wildcat Canyon Press publishes books that embrace such subjects as friendship, spirituality, women's issues, and home and family, all with a focus on self-help and personal growth. Great care is taken to create books that inspire reflection and improve the quality of our lives. Our books invite sharing and are frequently given as gifts.

Wildcat Canyon is an imprint of **Council Oak Books,** an independent publisher of quality books since 1984.